# How to Stop Trying

**Also by Kate Williams**

# How to Stop Trying

An Overachiever's Guide to
Self-Acceptance, Letting Go,
and Other Impossible Things

## Kate Williams

FLATIRON
BOOKS
NEW YORK

HOW TO STOP TRYING. Copyright © 2025 by Kate
Williams. All rights reserved. Printed in the
United States of America. For information,
address Flatiron Books, 120 Broadway, New York,
NY 10271.

www.flatironbooks.com

Designed by Donna Sinisgalli Noetzel

Library of Congress Cataloging-in-Publication Data

Names: Williams, Kate, 1980– author.
Title: How to stop trying : an overachiever's
    guide to self-acceptance, letting go, and other
    impossible things / Kate Williams.
Description: First edition. | New York : Flatiron
    Books, [2025]
Identifiers: LCCN 2024033281 | ISBN 9781250340900
    (hardcover) | ISBN 9781250340917 (ebook)
Subjects: LCSH: Self-acceptance. | Overachievement. |
    Women—Identity.
Classification: LCC BF575.S37 W55 2025 |
    DDC 158.1—dc23/eng/20241107
LC record available at https://lccn.loc.gov/2024033281

Our books may be purchased in bulk for
promotional, educational, or business use. Please
contact your local bookseller or the Macmillan
Corporate and Premium Sales Department at
1-800-221-7945, extension 5442, or by email at
MacmillanSpecialMarkets@macmillan.com.

First Edition: 2025

10  9  8  7  6  5  4  3  2  1

To all the overachievers.

Give yourself a break.

Gretchen, stop trying to make "fetch" happen!

It's not going to happen!

REGINA GEORGE, *MEAN GIRLS*

# Contents

# Contents

# How to Stop Trying

# Introduction

## These Trying Times

Have you ever heard anyone say, "I'm trying to make it work," and thought, *Ooh, that sounds good?* Or instantly chilled out when someone suggested you "try to relax"? Probably not. Because here's the thing about trying: it's tiring. Trying turns whatever you're doing into labor. If you've ever tried to have fun, tried to stay calm, or tried to fall asleep, you know exactly what I'm talking about. And yet, from the time we're children, many of us are bombarded with so many messages about how important it is to try that we have come to believe that trying is nonnegotiable. We believe that not trying again (even for the ninety-ninth time) is akin to failure. So we keep going. We never stop trying. And if all this trying exhausts us and saps our joy and makes us miserable, well then, we just try harder. Because, surely, the trying can't be the problem, we think. The problem is that we're not trying hard enough. The problem is us.

Wrong. *Wrong!* WRONG!

Sorry not sorry for shouting, but all this trying is infuriating because it's killing us, and we don't know how to stop. This is especially true for Gen X and millennial women (like me) who were the first generations raised with the belief that we could "have it all"—if we tried hard enough.

So we doubled down on trying from an early age. We didn't quit, pushed through pain, stayed positive, worked harder than everyone else, got shit done, refused to settle. We never let ourselves get comfortable, never stopped believing that we could do better and be better. And yet, no matter how hard we tried, no matter what we accomplished, we never felt like we really had it all. Instead, the more we proved what we could do, the more we were expected to do. The more we exceeded expectations, the greater they became, and now we're here, in an era of overachievement, a time when we're bombarded with messages that good enough isn't good enough anymore and that we must keep getting better.

I know lots of women who are doing amazing things. They are running companies and raising humans, making money, making homes, and making art. They are organizing and volunteering and cleaning and taking care of parents and taking care of children and taking care of themselves (when they can). They are doing yoga and HIIT and drinking less alcohol and more water and they are getting up in the morning and getting dressed and doing their hair and the laundry and the pickups and the drop-offs and sending memes to their friend who is going through a rough time and there is not a minute of the day that they are not maximizing in every way they can. They are strong, smart, compassionate, and incredible, and none of them feel like they are good enough.

They work so hard and yet feel like the only payoff is more work. To be a modern woman is to spend your whole life preparing for joy that you never actually get to experience, and then wondering what's wrong with you because of it. Now, here we are approaching middle age, or already smack-dab in it, and thinking the jig is up. The system is rigged and we can't go on like this.

Yet why is it that so much advice aimed at women focuses on what we can supposedly add to our to-do lists and busy days to help us better manage our to-do lists and busy days? Use a bullet journal. Wake up earlier. Get a side hustle. Get a standing desk. Clean your closet until it inspires joy. Put adaptogens in your oatmeal. Download this chore chart! Meal prep!! Plan a date night!!! Plan a night out with your friends!!!! Try to find balance, and OMG, why are you crying!?!

The subtext is always that we are doing it wrong, that we need someone to light a fire under our butts, but this couldn't be further from the truth. I don't know a single woman who is lacking in motivation or inspiration. I do know a lot of women who are lacking in sleep. So, as that lady from the '90s informercials used to say, we must *stop the insanity*.

It's time to break the cycle of nonstop self-improvement and goal obsession and recognize that trying to have (do, and be) it all often keeps you from having what you actually want—a happy, fulfilled life that you get to enjoy. We have to deprogram ourselves from the cultural conditioning that has convinced us that we're not enough so that we can reclaim our time and energy and live lives that align with our (and not everyone else's) priorities. We have to love ourselves as we are, right now, instead of believing we need to withhold that love a little bit longer, until we're perfect. We have to stop trying to be who we think we should be and let ourselves be who we are.

For the first four decades of my life, I tried hard, and a lot. From an early age, I was a classic type A overachiever. I prided myself on my determination, to-the-bone work ethic, and refusal to be satisfied.

Then five years ago, I started to pivot. I was thirty-nine, pregnant with my second child, and beginning to think that something was wrong because I no longer felt like shit.

In my first pregnancy, morning sickness had come on like a guerrilla ambush. I was familiar with the concept mostly from TV and movies, where pregnant characters were subject to cute and comical fits of morning barfing. That, I could have handled. What I got instead was a constant thrum of nausea that ebbed and flowed throughout the day. I was sick in the morning, but also in the afternoon and evening and sometimes in the middle of the night. The real kicker, though, was the exhaustion. I was used to being a workhorse, and now I was spent by 10:00 a.m. After an hour and a half of productivity, I could do nothing but lie on the couch. I couldn't even nap, because I always woke up feeling like I'd just been run over by a garbage truck.

But my second pregnancy was, of course, my second rodeo, and so when the exhaustion and the nausea came calling right around my sixth week, I was ready for them. I nibbled saltines, walked slowly, and did my best to clear my schedule. When trying to take a vitamin caused me to vomit up everything I'd painstakingly ingested, I even smiled. I knew that "morning sickness," in a lot of ways, was a sign of a healthy pregnancy, and so I could regard it as somewhat of a relief.

Then, just like that, it stopped.

I googled this and found nothing conclusive. *Everything is fine*, I told myself. *You're being paranoid.* Even when I started spotting blood, I continued with this "affirmation." After all, the internet was full of stories of women who spotted all through their first trimester and then still went on to have healthy babies. Besides, it was barely spotting—a faint wash of pink I only knew was there because I searched for it.

I was in a new city, with a new doctor, and my first appointment was still weeks away. Every time I thought about calling their office, I talked myself out of it. I didn't want to reveal myself as a high-maintenance, hypochondriac patient this early. When that appointment finally rolled around, I was so nervous on the drive there that I thought I might throw up. I interpreted this as a good sign, because maybe my morning sickness was coming back.

By the time I got into the exam room, I was sweating and shaky, and there was a good reason for that. It turned out that my intuition knew what my brain had been trying to override for weeks. The baby inside of me had stopped growing, probably right around the time I'd started to feel good. Everything was not fine.

The midwife who broke the news couldn't have

been nicer. She was concerned, comforting, and positive. This was a totally normal and healthy thing, she assured me. I'd gotten pregnant with my son quickly, and this pregnancy had come after only a couple of months of trying, and she had no doubt that I would be pregnant again in no time. *This is just a setback*, I told myself. *You have to keep trying.*

My husband and I had known plenty of people who had one child, who had only ever wanted one child, who hadn't wanted children at all, but that had never been us. On our first date in Los Angeles, we'd eaten tacos and sat under the fluorescent lights of the taqueria until long after the food was gone, playing Mexican love songs on the jukebox and talking about the kind of things you talk about on a first date when you just . . . know. My husband said he wanted five kids. I laughed—five seemed like a lot, but three had always seemed ideal to me.

So with this miscarriage, even though I was almost forty, I was sure we could make this happen. We just couldn't waste any time, and we had to focus ourselves 110 percent on our goal. Life, as it so often does, had other plans. For one, this was February 2020, and we all know what came next. Cue the masks, and the Purell, and the Clorox wipes, and the fear and the panic. Then, when I'd barely stopped bleeding from the miscarriage, we found out my husband needed emergency surgery. In addition to being terrifying for all the obvious reasons, this was also a logistical nightmare with a one-year-old. Our closest relative, my sister-in-law, drove nine hours so that she could take my husband to the hospital, where he needed to be at 4:30 in the morning. The doctor met him on the corner, in front of a Walgreens, to escort him into the hospital, and when he came out of the anesthesia, a nurse asked him what music he wanted to hear, then put it on the loudspeaker, since he was the only patient on the entire floor. The surgery went well, but for weeks after, I operated on pure adrenaline, sanitizing everything in sight to the point where I thought my fingertips might smell like bleach for the rest of my life.

Shortly after this ordeal, we decided that we needed to get out of the city, and we left San Francisco for my home state of Kansas. We packed our now two-year-old son and our pit bull in the car and headed east, wiping down motel rooms along the way. We bought a house, and, once settled, I published my second book and began fertility treatments in the form of ovulation-triggering drugs and intrauterine insemination. But the treatments didn't work. Then my husband had surgery again. By now, he could bring someone to the hospital with him, but only one person at a time, so I sat by myself while he was in the operating room, alternately scrolling TikTok and watching TV, wondering why every house renovated on HGTV turns out looking exactly the same. During his recovery, I was back in robot mode, doing what needed to be done and trying to allocate as little brain space as possible to thinking about how exhausted I was.

Two months after that, surprise! I was pregnant again, no treatments needed. Oh, happy day! But then, blood. Another miscarriage, this time, one that dragged on for several weeks as my hormone levels continued to rise. Not enough to sustain a pregnancy but just enough to make me feel like I was going to be sick in the middle of Target, a cosmic slap in the face when I was already trying very hard not to look over at the baby clothes.

That fall, I published my third novel, finished writing my fourth, ghostwrote a memoir, and we all got COVID. The following spring, I had my third miscarriage on my forty-second birthday. The babysitter was on the way, I was dressed to go out to dinner, and I lay down on the floor and sobbed.

What was once a minor setback had become a Sisyphean trek. So much climbing already and the mountain peak was still not in sight. I'd always prided myself on being a high-functioning doer who persisted no matter what, but now the rug had been pulled out from under me so many times that I was struggling to get back up. I'd been operating in crisis mode for years, and I was tired, so unbelievably tired. I knew I couldn't keep going. I couldn't try again. But I had to. If at first—er, twenty-seventh?—you don't succeed, right? In the aftershock of that third miscarriage (because even when it's not unexpected, it's still a shock), I did what I had always done: gritted my teeth and formulated a plan. "Okay," I told my husband a few nights after my birthday, as we sat on the couch, "I think we should spend the next month seriously considering all of our options, and then regroup and decide what to try next."

In my mind, I imagined spreadsheets that tracked the financials of IVF and adoption, tables that measured the pros and cons of everything from donor eggs to foster children, lists that gathered success rates, risks, potential emotional and physical tolls. I was going to approach this like I'd approached every other challenge in my life: with a potent cocktail of determination, hard work, and lots of Google Docs.

My husband listened as I outlined my plan, and he nodded. "I can do that," he said gently. "We can do that, but I think we both know what we really want to do."

I swallowed and nodded. "Nothing," I said.

"Yeah," he answered. "Nothing. We're not closing the door on it. We're just going to stop trying." *Stop trying.* I knew that was the right thing to do, but I had no idea how to do it.

So, once again, I did what one does in this situation—I turned to the internet for reassurance. I didn't get much. I wanted stories of women like me, who'd stopped trying to have a baby and still went on to lead happy, full lives, but I just couldn't find them. People always say that no one talks about miscarriage or infertility, but that's not really true. There are tons of stories out there, but most of them end in the same way: with a baby. There are plenty of stories that celebrate women who go to the ends of the earth to make their bundle-of-joy dreams come true but few about women who decide, when faced with an ending that's different from the one they imagined, to accept it and move on.

I understand why this is—when you're trying to have a baby, the last thing you want to read is a story about how it just never happened for someone because then that means that maybe it could never happen for you, too. The flip side to this is, of course, that if you find yourself in my situation, when you've decided the best thing to do is stop trying to live your dreams and instead make the most of your reality, you feel like you're the only one who's ever been there.

This sentiment wasn't just the dominant theme on the internet, either. When I began to share our decision with some of the people in my life, few congratulated me on making a hard choice that was the right one for our family. Instead, they offered their suggestions for other ways we could keep trying or regaled me with stories that they knew first-, second-, third-, and occasionally even friend's-neighbor's-cousin-hand that involved double-digit rounds of IVF, surrogacy, or trips halfway around the world to countries where such things were less expensive.

At first, I thought this at-all-costs determination was mostly about having children, but the more I searched, the more I started to see that this attitude and these beliefs—that one should never give up, keep trying no matter what, accept nothing less than everything you've ever wanted—were prevalent in every aspect of a woman's life. Sure, they were relayed in different ways, dressed in different fonts, conveyed in different inspirational tales, but the underlying intimation was always the same: You should want more because what you have now is not enough. You, yourself, are not enough, so you'd better keep trying until you are.

I so deeply bought into these beliefs that I'd made a career out of helping to sell them. I was born in 1980, right on the cusp of Generation X and millennials (if I were to illustrate this, it would be a picture of me playing *Oregon Trail* while wearing light pink), and I was a rabid consumer of pop culture and media from the time I discovered Madonna on MTV. I got my first magazine subscription, to *Teen*, right before middle school, and this planted a seed. Ten years later, I became a magazine editor, writing about beauty, fashion, and celebrities. I later worked as a copywriter, carefully crafting headlines and emails for fashion companies, and as a ghostwriter on celebrity memoirs and self-help books. Over the two decades of my career, no matter what I was writing, my audience has always been women. Much of what I've written has followed the same theme: telling women what to do and how to do it—be it a magazine article about how to get rid of acne, a marketing email about dressing on trend, or a memoir about how someone got where she is today through hard work and self-belief.

Now, looking back, I can see that it was all about trying. Trying to look better, trying to dress better, trying to feel better, trying to have more, do more, be more. Even breezy profiles of celebrities had the same message, it just wasn't quite as overt: Look how great she is! And see how she still isn't satisfied? See how she's still trying? No wonder I felt like I, too, always needed to try. I was clearly operating from inside a culture that believed that trying wasn't just the preferred option but the only one.

As someone who worked in the media, I always considered myself above being influenced by it. I knew what went into creating an image (Photoshop, stylist, hairdresser, makeup artist, duct tape, intern dispatched to Jamba Juice in a snowstorm, etc.), so I rarely looked at pictures of models or celebrities and thought, *My body should look like that.* Once I really started to think about it, though, I started to realize that I'd done something that was far more destructive. I'd always looked at the media I consumed and thought, *My life should look like that.* I thought that if I just kept trying, then maybe, someday, it would. I was mistaken, though. Life isn't just about trying. It's about living, and that starts with deciding that today is the day that you get to experience all that happiness and joy and ease and fulfillment that you've always denied yourself because you thought you hadn't quite earned it yet. Because you *have* earned it, and then some.

A lot of content for women is what we in the business call *prescriptive*, which is a fancy way of saying it is going to tell you what to do. I've always found this odd, that everything for women had to be crafted with the idea that we had no clue how to live our lives or do even the most basic things. Even when I worked at clothing brands, writing copy for marketing emails, the message was often something like "how to wear the new dress," and I'd want to pull my hair out because I'd think, *Oh my god, women aren't idiots! We know how to wear a dress—you pull it over your head and make sure your legs stick out of the bottom!!*

So this book is not going to talk to you like you're

clueless. As if. It's going to assume that you're a high-functioning human who has been doing hard things your entire life and now you just want to do a few easier ones. You know how you want to live, and so this book aims to help you cut through the infernal racket of modern life so you can actually do it.

I'm not writing this book because I have it all figured out. I'm writing this book because it's the book I need to read, and so I think it might be the book you need to read, too. In the following chapters, I'll show you how I stopped trying—to keep up with ridiculous expectations, to overextend myself, to convince myself that everything was okay when it wasn't. How I learned to let go of the way I thought things should be so that I could move on from the past and relax about the future, and even have a little fun along the way. This book is not about sticking a Band-Aid on the wound and convincing yourself it doesn't hurt anymore. This is a book about healing. Sometimes healing is easier said than done, but when were you ever scared of a little hard work? Never. Literally, never. So, get in, winner; we're going to stop trying.

# 1
---

# Just Stop Swimming

All my friends were doing it, so the summer after my freshman year of high school, I decided I was going to do it, too. There's a first time for everything, after all, so I joined the swim team.

The swim team met at our community pool, and some of my friends had already been competing for years and could do ridiculous swimming things, like an entire one hundred meters of the butterfly. From watching them, I could see that there were definite perks to being on the swim team—namely, meeting swimmers from other pools (read: cute boy swimmers) and getting to hang out with the lifeguards and swim coaches, who were all cool high school grads and college students. I definitely wanted to avail myself of those perks, and I was a strong recreational swimmer, so when a couple of friends who'd also never competed before decided to join, I enthusiastically signed up with them.

As a teenager, I considered 11:50 a.m. to be the morning, and I relished summer because it was three long months of sleeping in. Swim team practice was at 9:00 a.m., which was not ideal. Even still, when my mom dropped me off that first day, I was excited. I also had no idea what I was in for. I had never swum back and forth from one end of the pool to the other nonstop for an hour. Later, that afternoon, I walked the aisles of the grocery store and realized my arms were so sore I could barely raise them over my head. The pain made me proud. I didn't just swim, *I was a swimmer*.

But by the end of the first week, this sense of satisfaction had worn off, because being a swimmer wasn't getting any easier. It was the opposite, in fact, as practices got harder to accommodate for the fact that we were supposed to be getting used to the workouts. My friends quit before we even had our first meet. "Practice is the same time as *The Price Is Right*," one guy explained, which, in the days of live television, was a very solid reason. Even though I was chlorine green with envy, I hung in there, plunging into the cold deep end every morning seething with bitterness about missing Sharon from Sheboygan, or whoever was today's lucky contestant, come on down to have a spin at the Big Wheel.

I dreaded that first swim meet. The night before, I was so nervous I couldn't sleep. The morning of, so nervous I couldn't eat. I stood at the edge of the pool awaiting the start of the race like I was awaiting my own execution. The gun sounded, and as soon as I dove in, my goggles filled with water. Shocked and disoriented, I immediately stood up and ripped them off my head. The shrill blast of a whistle directed at me—disqualified for touching the bottom of the pool. A common occurrence with the elementary school set, less so among the teenagers.

This was the beginning of June. Swim season lasted until August, and each meet went something like the first. Disqualified for not actually touching the wall during a flip turn. Swimming a 100-meter breaststroke with my goggles at my throat like a necklace. Being the literal anchor on the relay. Finishing so last that the other swimmers were already wrapped in towels by the time I touched the wall. Finishing so, *so* last that I got a sincere round of applause—from the other team's parents.

Everyone knew I was bad. My badness at swimming was accepted as a fact and openly discussed. "My mom says your stroke is good," said my friend Chris, who had qualified for the state championships. "You're just super slow." Being on the swim team made me miserable and had turned my summer from a blissful expanse of reruns and cherry limeades into weekly humiliation spectacles. But I kept swimming.

For years, I told this story anytime I was applying for something—in scholarship essays, during sorority rush, at job interviews—because I was proud of it. In my mind, the Summer I Joined the Swim Team story illustrated that, even from a young age, I was not someone who gave up! But I share it now for the opposite reason—I don't look back at that girl and feel proud. Instead, I feel sad for her.

As she labors, slowly and miserably, through the 100-meter freestyle, I see evidence of a pattern woven throughout the first four decades of her life, of *my* life: I didn't keep going because I wanted to, but because I was scared to quit. I was scared that quitting would mean that *I was a quitter*, that I was letting people down, and besides, we all know what they say about quitters. Cue the Beck: *Soy un perdedor*...I was not going to be a loser. I was going to hang in there, no matter what. Gasp, glug, sputter, sink.

I don't remember specifically where I learned that winners never quit, and that if at first you don't succeed, you should try again (and again, and again). These were things I always knew. Everybody knew, because these ideas were everywhere. And just like I can't pinpoint where I'd first heard these ideas, I also can't pinpoint where, or who, exactly they came from, though I can find a billion examples of famous, important people putting their own spin on them. "The main thing is never quit, never quit, never quit," said Bill Clinton. Mike Ditka puts it this way: "You're never a loser until you quit trying." "The most certain way to succeed is to try just one more time," said none other than Thomas Edison.

I haven't bothered to try to find out if any of these people really said these things, because honestly, it doesn't matter. These ideas are so big and so important to our culture that we automatically assume they must have come from, or at least be shared by, people equally important—presidents, coaches, inventors, and other mythic (and male) godlike figures.

Now, I can look back and see that I took the idea of not quitting to heart because I was using it to make a point. When I refused to quit, I was proving myself. I was proving that I was tough, determined, that I didn't expect anything to be easy or given to me, that I could hang in there even when it made me miserable, or especially when it made me miserable.

One day, while in the midst of thinking about this very thing, I was in a museum and came face-to-face with a little girl, probably eight or nine, wearing a hot-pink T-shirt that said GIRLS DON'T QUIT. It was a startling reminder of how early, and explicitly, this narrative starts. Is it only words on a shirt, or a message that this little girl will take to heart, a phrase she will one day repeat to herself as she continues to put her all into something that hurts her? "Girls don't quit" isn't an encouragement, it's an order. A reminder that, if you're a girl, quitting is just one more thing you are not allowed to do.

And why is that? Why is it so important for us to learn that we can't quit something that is making us miserable? Could it be because this world needs us to stick with stuff we don't want to do, with stuff nobody wants to do, because who else is going to do it? Probably not men.

As girls, we learn not to quit the swim team, and as grown women, we learn not to quit the many other things that make us unhappy. We stick with it, even when "it" is a committee we don't have the time for, emotional labor that exhausts us, responsibilities that are outside our job description, projects we never wanted to do in the first place, or chores that go unnoticed by everyone else in our household (the towels wash themselves, right?).

We are meant to internalize the idea that people who quit do so because they are weak, lazy, or stupid.

Maybe even all three! They can't stand a little discomfort, and so they give up as soon as they're faced with something that might be uncomfortable, painful, or even just plain boring. People quit, we think, because they don't have what it takes, and what it takes is a willingness to do whatever it takes. "Whatever it takes" can be defined the same way as obscenity—you know it when you see it. Maybe it's long hours, or cold calls, or pay cuts, or sleepless nights, but whatever it takes is always a sacrifice.

While it is true that you quite often have to sacrifice something to get what you want, in the adrenaline-fueled echo chamber that we currently live in, we've come to think that no sacrifice is too big. Burnout is seen as a socially acceptable form of self-immolation, especially for women, who are so conditioned to believe that mental and physical pain is normal we often don't even notice that we're on fire until we've already turned to ash. I always thought I couldn't quit until I'd absolutely obliterated myself, because any bits of me that weren't charred beyond repair were just proof that I still had more to give, that I still hadn't tried hard enough.

These beliefs came on full force after my third miscarriage, because there were still plenty of baby-making options left on the table, and I was reminded of that constantly. I'd considered all of them, but when

I even started to think about the rigors of IVF or the complications of the adoption process, I became physically ill. Yet I still felt I had to do something, that I couldn't quit *yet*.

My husband had made it clear that this was ultimately my decision, so no matter how overwhelmed I got just thinking about it, I continued to do so. When I discussed IVF with my doctor, he was positive about the physical aspects, but less so about the emotional ones. "Physically, your body recovers pretty quickly," he said. "But people who choose to do IVF usually do so because they believe that it will work, and it can be very devastating when it doesn't."

I asked my therapist what she thought, and she was less diplomatic. "It can be very dangerous," she said, her words uncharacteristically charged with emotion. "Maybe not physically, but it is incredibly hard mentally and emotionally, especially on women who have a history of anxiety or depression." This gave me pause because the whole reason I was seeing her was because I had a history of anxiety and depression.

But still, even after this, I tried to think about how I could swing it. Maybe it wouldn't be so hard if I never expected it to work? But then, if I never expected it to work, why was I going to do it in the first place? Just because I wanted to believe that I had tried everything? I was battling with myself because I thought that if

I wasn't willing to do whatever it took, then I clearly didn't deserve the baby. It's almost as if I thought they were handed out like extra credit, like the universe would see how hard I was working and say, "Great job persevering, Kate. Here are some twins."

I had to face the truth: When it came to having another baby, I was not actually willing to do whatever it took. What I was willing to do was move on. So we quit trying. For weeks afterward, I felt a little bit like I didn't know what to do with myself, but I also began to feel a subtle weight being lifted. There was no longer anything to do, no decisions to turn over and over in my head until my brain felt raw, no hope to cling to by the tips of my fingernails. I could stop structuring my life around what I might have someday (another baby) and start to refocus my energy on what I already had today—an incredible child, a strong marriage, an inspiring career, to name a few. I no longer had to constantly measure myself and my life by what I didn't have.

Don't get me wrong—there are plenty of times in our lives when we have to hang on and when refusing to quit is a good thing. But not every time is one of those times, and often, we end up continuing to pursue our goal and refusing to quit out of habit. When the going gets tough, sometimes hanging in there helps you survive. Other times, it just keeps you stuck, and in these instances, the only way to move forward is to let go.

Hanging in there brings to mind a cute little kitten clinging to a branch, a ubiquitous image from any '70s or '80s childhood, and I think it's actually a perfect image to illustrate not why you should hang in there, but why you shouldn't. That little kitten is hanging in there because she's scared. We're supposed to look at the fear and pain in her eyes and think that it is better for her to stay there than to risk whatever is below, even though we have no idea what's outside the frame. Maybe it's a twenty-foot plunge into rocks and broken glass, or maybe it's just a gentle drop into marshmallows and feather pillows. But even if it is a hard fall, cats have nine lives. No matter what happens, if that little kitten lets go, she'll be fine. She might even land on her feet. You might, too.

We often think that hanging in there "builds character," which is essentially a way of saying that we are getting used to doing things we don't want to do now so that we may do more of them later. Yes, there's always a chance that first impressions will not prove correct and that you may begin to like, or even love, something if you stick with it, and this is especially true with kids. Maybe it's a good idea to give something a second chance, or even a third, but if you still aren't sold on the fourteenth try, it's unlikely that the fifteenth is going to be any different.

We are often loath to give up on something because

of the time, effort, and money we have already put in. "Already paid for it" is a reason you often hear for why people think they "can't quit now," as if getting their money's worth is more important than enjoying themselves. This is sound reasoning if there is a guarantee that they'll be rewarded for their efforts, but it is important to remember that there are no guarantees. With anything. Ever. The work itself might be the only reward you're going to get, so if all your trying adds up to a hill of beans, will it at least be enough to make chili?

If pursuing a goal makes you feel energized, and if you get excited not just thinking about the end but also about all the work it will take to get there, then by all means, keep going! But if the pursuit and the work are making you exhausted, if you're dreading your day-to-day, and if you just can't wait until the whole thing is over, maybe it's time to ask yourself if you want to keep at it. And yes, we all have those days, the bad days, but if the bad days have totally occluded the good, then maybe you are sacrificing too much.

The truth is that winners are not people who don't quit. Winners are people who know when to quit, and you'll probably find that, when you actually get the chance to listen to yourself, this is you. You know when to quit. So, if you know when to quit, but still aren't doing it, it's probably because you have some ideas about what it means to be "a quitter." If you take the time to really examine these ideas, they often don't hold up because they aren't, and never were, your ideas in the first place. The narrative that quitting is bad is not something that you came to on your own. Instead, it was drilled into you by individuals and institutions who needed you to keep going, not for your own benefit but for theirs. It's a lot easier to give up the ideas you've been carrying around for years when you realized they didn't even belong to you in the first place. You can put them down, throw them in the trash, or set them on fire—whatever it takes to make space for new ideas and new beliefs, ones that will better serve you and help you get closer to what you really want out of life.

Often, when we examine the thing that we are working for, the goal that we are pursuing, we find that what we want is not so much *the thing* as it is how we think *the thing* will make us feel. We want the job, the relationship, the house, the child, the bank account because we believe that, once we have it, we'll be happy. We believe that, with *the thing* firmly in our pocket, we will finally feel good about ourselves.

The irony here is that the very process of pursuing what we think will make us feel better often just makes us feel worse. Instead of building our lives around what we have, we center them on what we don't. We constantly remind ourselves of what we lack. We endure the hell of today, even when we don't have to, because of the remote possibility that doing so might lead to heaven tomorrow. We exist in a state of permanent suspension, constantly sacrificing the concrete reality of the present for the vague hope of the future. Pain is not always a sign of imminent gain— sometimes it just means something hurts.

Quitting is not for cowards. It takes a lot of courage to cut your losses and admit that something might not happen, to brush yourself off and not try again. It takes even more to admit that you still want something even though you are not willing to do whatever it takes to get it. Quitting can be a huge demonstration of self-love, because it shows that you value your life right now, rather than thinking of it as merely a disposable stepping stone on the path to a life you think is better. Giving up on your goals does not mean that you are giving up on yourself. In fact, you have to really believe in yourself to give up on a goal, because you have to believe that you don't need to achieve more to be worthy.

Being able to quit is a sign that you are in touch with your priorities and that you are ready to stop doing all those things you no longer want to do so that you have more time to do the things that you actually enjoy. Quitting doesn't mean that you are weak. Often it means that you are strong.

So, go forth, fair maiden, and quit. Quit jobs, quit relationships. Quit teams and committees, quit plans and courses and strategies and resolutions. Quit anything that is making you miserable. When you find yourself thinking, *I can't go on like this*, ask yourself if you really have to. If the answer is no, then you know what to do.

You can quit now, knowing that there will inevitably be more times in your life when you have to keep going, when you have to hang on until your hands are raw, when you have to try one more goddamn time. When that time comes, you won't quit. You'll swim for your life. Until then, you can get out of the water, and go lie in the sun.

# 2

## Internalized Misogyny
## Is a Real Bitch

The first strip club I ever went to was called the Outhouse, and it was as classy as its name might suggest. A few miles into the country on a bumpy dirt road outside of the town where I went to college, the Outhouse had once been a legendary punk venue that hosted shows by bands such as Nirvana, Sonic Youth, and Green Day, but by the time I visited in the early 2000s, it was an all-nude, BYOB kind of place. The Outhouse stayed open until four in the morning, when all the surrounding bars closed at two, which was how I found myself headed there, late one night, in a caravan headed by two of my closest guy friends.

These guys were a couple of years older than I was and both worked for a local concert promoter booking shows. On this particular night, we'd all been at one of their events, a raucous dance party helmed by an out-of-town DJ who was ready to go out now that his own show had ended. As his hosts, my friends wanted to show him a good time, and everyone knew there was only one place to go. After packing a cooler with beers from the venue's bar, my friends offered to drop me back at my apartment on the way. "Does this mean I'm not invited?" I asked.

"No, you're invited," one of them said. "Do you want to go?"

"Hell yes, I want to go!" I said. I was being totally sincere and enthusiastically piled in the car, the only girl in our party aside from one I'd never met, who I took to be the DJ's girlfriend. I'd never been to a strip club before, and I was excited to see what it was all about, especially since I wanted to make it clear that I was "not the kind of girl" who looked down on, or was made uncomfortable by, strippers.

When we arrived at the Outhouse, I was not disappointed. It was a fascinating study in humanity and also, in my opinion, a totally unsexy environment. I was made more comfortable by the fact that my friends hung back and people-watched with me. (Yes, that is a guy getting change back from a lap dance. On a twenty!!!) When someone came around carrying a giant bucket, soliciting donations for the jukebox, my friend pointed out that there was no jukebox before throwing a couple of dollars in the bucket. Within twenty minutes of arriving, I was telling anyone who would listen that I thought the strippers were the only respectable ones in the whole place.

I was having a grand old time demonstrating how cool and unbothered I was by this crazy scene, but grew worried about the DJ's girlfriend, who seemed kind of quiet and unengaged as she watched him get a lap dance. I decided that, girl to girl, it was my job to make her feel as comfortable as I was, and so I moved over to sit next to her and chat her up. As I made small talk, though, it dawned on me that my impression of who she was and why she was there was totally wrong. She wasn't the DJ's girlfriend but a girl he had met hours earlier, a girl who was going to go home with a guy who first took her to a strip club and ignored her. I excused myself and went back to sit with my friends. "Who is she?" I asked, and one of them shrugged.

"I don't know," he said. "She came up to him as we were leaving and said she wanted to go back to the hotel with him." I nodded and decided not to talk to her for the rest of the night. We were not the same. I was not that kind of girl.

For a long time, the irony of this was lost on me—how I could be so righteous about respecting strippers because sex work is work, but look down on some-one who I presumed was going to hook up with a DJ simply because . . . she wanted to? This memory surfaced recently when I started to unpack the idea of internalized misogyny. It really stood out to me because it was such a blatant incident of slut-shaming, but mostly because it's one of the few instances I can recall where my internalized misogyny was, in hindsight, so cut-and-dried and obvious. I have been blind to how embodied sexism shaped my perception of other women and of myself for most of my life, and long after I could write it off as youthful ignorance.

Having grown up in a misogynistic society (thank you, patriarchy!), I've spent my life categorizing other women, and their behavior, as good or bad. Most of the time, I thought nothing of it. Rather, it seemed normal and natural to apply these same good/bad classifications to myself and everything I did as well. Misogyny, both external and internal, leads us to believe that women should behave a certain way (good) and that those who do not should feel ashamed about it (bad). It teaches us that certain characteristics and behaviors are more valuable in women than others and uses societal pressures to enforce these unwritten rules. This is where we get slut-shaming, fat-shaming, age-shaming, mom-shaming, victim-shaming, and a whole host of other behaviors that are employed to make women feel generally inferior to men yet superior to one another. Misogyny leaves us always trying to be the right kind of girl—the good girl—while distancing ourselves from the bad. However, no matter how good we try to be, no matter how much distance we put between ourselves and those who are bad, we still never feel good enough—because we don't get to define what makes a woman good. Men do. A good woman is a woman men want. We're taught to see male approval as the highest form of achievement available to a woman. In everything from fairy tales to contemporary rom-coms, when we see a heroine who's found her happily ever after, we're not just seeing a woman in love—we're seeing a woman who has won.

Having internalized misogyny does not mean that we are subservient, anti-feminist, uneducated, or any other pejoratives that we might wish to sling at ourselves because we are so used to both dishing out and taking criticism. Sadly, it usually means that we are normal, the product of cultural conditioning that is subtle and subliminal, and also extremely effective.

The fact that many of us operate on at least a little bit of embodied sexism is a hard pill to swallow, especially for Gen X and millennial women who were raised by feminists and surrounded by messages of equality. But those messages always had a subtext: if someone has to go out of their way to tell you that you are equal, then you probably aren't. After all, no one took time out and made a special effort to make sure the boys knew that they could do anything girls could do, and damned if we didn't notice.

I had always prided myself on being "one of the guys" because this felt like its own kind of achievement. When I was a kid, this was easy to prove—all I had to do was endure such indignities as earthworms dropped down the back of my shirt, deliberate farts in my vicinity, and once being smacked in the back of the head with a live carp that someone chucked at me from a distance. As I got older, hanging out with the boys became less about the ability to dodge airborne aquatic animals and more about distinguishing myself as a girl friend and not a girlfriend. The main thing, no matter what age, was to not do girly things. Like get mad, or get upset, or cry, or really do anything other than just go with the flow. I remember one night as a teenager, the only girl hanging out with a group of guys, when I must have broken this unwritten rule. I don't remember the specifics of what I said, but I do remember how they responded: by chanting "Send the bitch home!"

I also learned that while I had to try hard to prove myself equal to the boys, I had to be careful about ever proving myself better. I remember once in high school history, the teacher announced that I'd gotten the best test score in the class. Irate and disbelieving, a male classmate demanded that my score be recounted, and so the teacher handed him the answer key and my test, and let him do it himself in front of the entire class. That the teacher meant well didn't change the fact that the whole thing was uncomfortable and kind of embarrassing, because I, and everyone else in the room, knew that the whole reason my score had been made a big deal of in the first place was that the teacher considered it an anomaly.

It's experiences like this that teach us, at an early age, how to police ourselves. We learn that we can't just be—we have to be a certain way. Rather than taking our inherent form, we have to mold ourselves into the preapproved, girl-shaped one that's available to us. That's why we're so good at trying—it is all that we know. Most of our trying isn't even about trying to achieve a goal or make a dream come true but trying to change the very fabric of who we are into what we think we should be. This means every moment of your life requires work and effort to try to be good. And we wonder why we're so tired!

We try to make ourselves small, so as not to offend, but also must always try to be the bigger person, so as to be unoffendable (of course I laughed in the face of "Send the bitch home," but I still remember it thirty years later). We should be able to meet everyone else's needs while also understanding that if our needs aren't met, it's our bad for having needs in the first place. While men are able to channel their trying and effort into growth and expansion, we must do the opposite. We must be capable but not bossy, perfectionists with ourselves but wholly accepting of others' flaws (as long as they're male), and when we do manage to win some sort of approval, we must accept it with a level of gratitude that borders on groveling. Eighty-four cents for every dollar? We're not worthy, we're not worthy, we're not worthy . . .

Even though I've always tried hard to be good, from an early age, I always had an inherent understanding that I was bad. I knew I was bad because I wanted, and good girls didn't want, at least not things that they didn't already have or that someone else wasn't already offering. Wanting made me inconvenient, and so I heard the words "get with the program" a lot. Eventually, I learned that if I wanted something—whether it was dressing a certain way or being treated a certain way—I couldn't possibly ask for it. I had to work the back channels, make sure that everyone around me knew that the only reason I wanted something was because it was good for everyone, not just me, and that giving it to me had been their idea in the first place. The catch-22 of this approach is that it only further convinced me of my own badness, because then I saw myself as manipulative, too. After all, when we're not allowed to be straightforward about our wants, needs, or feelings, guess what we become? Crafty, scheming, "nasty" women. Our aggression can only be passive or else, watch out, major B-word label coming our way!

We train ourselves into being who and what we think other people want us to be as a survival technique. Just like we've seen good girls be rewarded, we've seen the bad ones punished. Sometimes we've even helped punish them ourselves. Sure, we're no longer throwing women in the stocks with a scarlet letter sewn onto their chests, but women who don't conform still become the subjects of gossip and ridicule and bullying and exclusion. We rarely think anything is wrong with these kind of behaviors because we grow up around gossip in our communities and families, and we also exist in a culture where it's institutionalized in the media. Sometimes it's dressed up as an intellectual think piece or even as a public service in the name of feminism (let's rip her apart because what she is doing is bad for all of us!), but anytime a woman's choices are being discussed and dissected without her consent, well, let's just say you can put a viral peel-off lip stain on a pig all you want but it's still going to oink. And who wants to be the target of that pig, even if its lip color lasts all day? Not me, and probably not you, either.

We also see how women are punished when they

screw up. When men make mistakes, they are usually regarded as just that—mistakes. With women, though, we tend to interpret their mistakes as evidence of their overall badness, and slap labels on them—*hysterical, slut, bitch, crazy, inept, flaky*—that they then can't shake off.

Of all the ways internalized misogyny affects the way you view and treat other women, the real victim of your inflated expectations, harsh judgments, and cruel punishments will be yourself. If you have spent your entire life struggling to believe that your worth lies in the simple fact that you exist and not in what you do and how you act and how much others value your goodness, it is very difficult to change that wiring—especially when doing so often results in being gaslit by a patriarchal society that knows that the best way to keep women struggling is to deny the struggle exists at all. Whadda ya mean women have it rough? What about all those ladies' nights when you got into the club FOR FREE?! Do you know how much money you have saved by being a lady?! (Approximately seventeen dollars amortized over a lifetime of butt grabs and strangers standing too close on the subway, but hey, who's counting?) Don't ever let anyone convince you that the struggle is not real. It's about as real as it gets.

I've always had the impression that I couldn't just show up; I had to make sure I brought something to the table. I mean this in a literal way, in that I would rather eat alone at a combination Taco Bell / Pizza Hut that was next to the bathroom in a bus station than show up to a dinner party empty-handed. But I also mean this in the way that I felt my value was determined by external factors, like what I had accomplished, what I could do for someone else, or how much others approved of what I was doing. It seemed natural to me that my baseline was going above and beyond because I always felt like the standards were different for me. The reason I felt like this was because—get this!—they were. I was absolutely, 100 percent getting judged more harshly than my male peers. And when, in turn, I turned that harsh glare of judgment on myself, or other women, I did it in the name of trying to be good, and tried to ignore the fact that it all made me feel so bad.

So, what do we do here? How do we start to dismantle a way of thinking that has infused every aspect of our existence with trying? Not by blaming the victim (you and her) or pointing fingers (at you or her), because that's just adding fuel to the misogynistic fire. Instead, we start with simply being aware of the fact that embodied sexism has likely affected our self-perception and our worldview, and we give ourselves a break. While this might sound small—and a lot like doing nothing, especially to doers who are used to taking action—it's actually monumental because it requires bucking off a lifetime of conditioning meant to keep us locked in the cycles of judgment that go hand in hand with trying. When you're able to take a step back and get some distance, you'll likely be able to see that the constant categorization that internalized misogyny encourages has been a huge drain on your energy, and that it's taken up far too much of your brain space for far too long. Instead of putting time and effort into trying to figure out who's good and who's bad, and where you fit in on that continuum, you can just get on with your life.

Talking about how someone else is bad might make you feel good for a hot minute, but schadenfreude has a worse hangover than a box of red wine, and it's just not worth it. The less time and energy you invest in caring about what other people do, the less time and energy you will invest in caring about what they think of you. When you no longer feel like you need to police yourself all the time, you'll feel less of a need to police other people. When you stop judging other people, a magical thing will happen: you'll stop judging yourself. You do not need to try to be a kind of way or act a kind of way or look a kind of way. You do not have to try so hard to be a good girl. All you have to do is be a good person, and that's much easier. There are so many fewer rules! Internalized misogyny is not the only force that keeps us locked in patterns of believing that we are inherently bad and unworthy, but it is one of the most powerful, and freeing yourself of that feels like finally shedding existential Spanx. You do not have to resign yourself to smallness. You can be big. You can be bold. You can even, if you want, be bad, and you might just find that it feels . . . good.

# 3

## Main Character Energy

I began to plan for motherhood as soon as I saw those two pink lines on my home pregnancy test, and everything I read, watched, or listened to drove home the importance of breastfeeding. According to everyone, it was the absolute best thing that you could do for your baby, and since *the best* was exactly what I wanted for my future child, I was going to crush breastfeeding like the competition that I was sure it was. I read books and watched videos and took classes. I was 100 percent confident that I had at least one, if not two, Lactater of the Year trophies in my future. At least, right up until I actually tried it.

At birth, my son was a healthy nine pounds and hungry for more. My body—wrecked from a grueling labor and hours of pushing and vomiting before an eventual C-section—had nothing to give him. His blood sugar kept dropping, and we were told we needed to supplement with formula. I could barely speak at this point, but I was skeptical. Nowhere, in any of my breastfeeding preparation, had I come across the idea that formula might ever be necessary. Formula was a choice that some women took when they were looking for an easy way out. I certainly wasn't one of *those* moms—I knew that breastfeeding was going to be a lot of work, and I was ready for it. The nurse patiently assured me that it was, indeed, necessary sometimes and that this was one of those times. It was also, she said, likely only temporary, and she assured me that I would be able to breastfeed exclusively once my milk came in. I was relieved that I would still be able to be the kind of mom I wanted to be—a breastfeeding mom. Aka, a good mom.

Flash forward, several days. Home from the hospital and my milk had come in. Except there wasn't that much of it. With several forced deep breaths, I told myself there was hardly reason to panic—yet. In the breastfeeding world, there exists a special kind of superhero called the lactation consultant, and according to lore, she is magical, mythical, all-knowing, all-seeing, and can fix almost any problem that involves both a baby and breasts. So I flashed the giant boob signal into the sky, and she arrived.

Rather, I sent an email, but she responded quickly, and within a few hours, a stranger was sitting on my couch, squeezing my nipples as I sat topless next to her on a Friday night. Surreality of this experience aside, I was glad to have her there. She weighed my son before and after he ate, and assured me that my milk supply was fine. So fine, in fact, that I didn't need to supplement with formula at all. I could start exclusively breastfeeding and be a formula mom no more!

And yet, my son still seemed hungry all the time. Hungrier, even, now that he wasn't getting supplemental formula. Come Monday, even though she had my phone number, the lactation consultant sent me an email. She had just discovered that the scale she had used to weigh my son before and after he ate, which provided her with the evidence that he was getting enough food, had been set to weigh in grams, not ounces. I was definitely not producing enough milk, and he was definitely not getting enough food, and so the reason he seemed so hungry was because . . . he was.

Sobbing and angry (You had one job! One job!!), I frantically made my son a bottle, but still felt determined not to resign myself to this formula fate. I quickly found a new lactation consultant, and when she arrived, she confirmed what I suspected: I wasn't producing enough milk. She helpfully suggested that this was a problem I could easily fix. All I had to do was tape a small surgical plastic tube to my nipple and run the tube to a bottle of formula. That way, I could supplement without my son becoming used to bottles and deciding he preferred them. With this, and extra pumping, my supply would increase in no time.

So, I commenced with the surgical tube. It was awkward and messy and was a whole thing, and soon it became clear that my son and I weren't going anywhere. I could breastfeed in public or give my son a bottle in public, but I couldn't tape a tube to my boob in public, so in our overstuffed chair we sat. Our days were consumed with nursing. More specifically, trying to nurse, but mostly pumping and taping tubes and sterilizing so many plastic parts in hot water that my fingertips burned and blistered.

When I was still hardly making any milk after weeks of tube-taping and constant pumping, my lactation consultant seemed confused and unsure of where to go next. Eventually, she suggested I start taping tubes to both boobs. I never called her again, and she never followed up with me, either. After several more weeks trying to breastfeed around the clock, two more lactation consultants, and nonstop crying (mainly by me), I took my son to the pediatrician for a regular checkup. As it happened, we were assigned to see a different doctor from our usual. This pediatrician, a warm, gray-haired man that everyone called Dr. John, patiently listened while I shared every detail of my breastfeeding saga. Unlike the previous doctor I'd seen, he didn't offer suggestions for how I could keep trying. Instead, he simply looked at me and said, "How does all of this make you feel?"

I was stunned. In the three months that I'd been frantically trying to breastfeed, no one had ever asked me how I felt. No one had even suggested that it mattered, and so I had assumed that it did not. I answered Dr. John honestly. "Awful," I said. "I feel absolutely awful."

He smiled and nodded. "Then stop," he said. "This isn't only about your baby. You need to be happy and healthy, too. There is absolutely nothing wrong with formula." I walked out of that appointment with a weight lifted. For the first time since my son was born, I had hope that maybe I could be a good mother after all, and if what was best for my son was to have a happy mother, then happy I would be!

Happiness, however, proved elusive. No longer hungry all the time, my son now slept through the night, but I did not. I lay awake in bed, gripped with anxiety and to-do lists and self-doubt, until, exhausted, I'd finally pass out for a couple of hours in the early morning. Everyone had always told me that things got better, and easier, as the baby got older, but for me, they were getting worse. I had failed at breastfeeding. I'd taken the easy way out, and I still wasn't happy.

Finally, I decided to go see my doctor, but since it was more than a week before she had an opening, I opted to see a nurse practitioner instead. At the appointment, I explained that I was looking for a therapist, but in the meantime, I desperately needed something to help me sleep, to get out of the insomnia loop that made me start to panic as soon as the sun went down.

She was unmoved by my distress. "You're not worried you won't wake up if your baby needs you?" she asked. I assured her I was not, that I was a light sleeper, and that my husband was always there anyway. "Are you breastfeeding?" she asked. I gave her the rundown, and that the baby mostly ate formula, because I'd never produced enough milk, and that I was probably going to stop trying to breastfeed at all anymore because the whole ordeal had been so hard on me. She scowled as she placed her stethoscope to my chest to listen to my heart.

"You shouldn't stop breastfeeding," she said. "It's what is best for your baby." I wondered if she could hear my heartbeat kick up at the fear that I'd made a mistake and revealed myself to be a bad mom and now she wasn't going to give me the prescription. I swallowed, hoping to backtrack.

"I know," I said, quickly and softly. "You're right. I'll keep trying."

So, that's what I did, right up until my breast pump broke a few weeks later. When I fired up my reserve pump, it didn't work, either. Already out hundreds of dollars in breast pumps, I ordered a used one from eBay, but by the time it arrived, it was too late. My milk was gone. I finally had to admit that I had failed. "You can always just tell people that it's breast milk in a bottle," my mom said. She meant this as a helpful suggestion, but the meaning was clear. I had become *that kind* of mom, so the least I could do was try to keep it a secret.

And, so I did.

My son was six months old at the time, and while feeding was no longer as complicated and fraught as it had been, I still avoided most situations where we'd have to do it in public. I didn't want anyone (even a stranger) to see me whip out a bottle, for fear they'd think I was a selfish parent. I steered clear of mom groups and even individual mothers who had babies around the same age. Basically any place or situation where the small talk might veer toward breastfeeding. When my son was nine months old, I posted a pic of him to Instagram and considered deleting it after I noticed that there was a bottle visible in the background. The day he turned one—the official age when the

American Academy of Pediatrics says it's okay to stop breastfeeding—I felt like I could come out of hiding and start fresh.

I couldn't shake the guilt, though, that maybe my problem was that I hadn't tried hard enough or tried in the right ways. One day, months later, I sat down and made a list of everything I had done to make breast-feeding work. I listed every tip, trick, and hack, every expert I'd consulted, every supplement I'd taken, recipe I'd made, every piece of equipment I'd purchased, and so on and so forth. When I was done, my list was four pages long. Single spaced.

There, written out in front of me in black and white, was proof that I hadn't just tried—I'd gone off the rails with trying. For those months, trying was all I did. I didn't eat, sleep, rest, see friends, exercise, or allow myself to do anything enjoyable, and I was miserable and falling apart because of it. I didn't question this, though, because I thought suffering was part of my job, as a woman and definitely as a mom. Good moms sacrificed, and more than anything, I wanted to be a good mom.

Part of the reason I was so worried about being a good mom was because in addition to having a baby that I loved, I also had a career that I cared a lot about, a career that was the fruition of all that child-hood wanting that I knew, deep down, was part of what made me bad. Having a career I loved meant there would be more than one priority in my life— and I didn't have a lot of role models for what this looked like. In pop culture, career women were often portrayed as frigid bitches or as innocents who cared about their jobs only because they hadn't yet realized what was really important (motherhood!). Growing up, I knew plenty of women who worked, but there was also an unspoken distinction between those who had "jobs" and those who had "careers." Jobs were something that you didn't like, that you did just for the money. You took a job so that you could help your family. Careers, on the other hand, were a hindrance to your family, even when they came with a paycheck, and I often heard gossip about women who had ca- reers. *Can you believe she hired a babysitter on Friday when she already hadn't seen her kids all week?* Stories about career women were told with an emphasis on the ways they had failed—like an older sibling drop- ping a child off for a playdate without a coat, in the middle of winter—and the unspoken implication was always that a woman who pursued a career must not have her priorities in order.

In the months leading up to my son's birth, I en- countered scrutiny about the fact that I was looking for childcare because I still hoped to meet a book dead- line. "You know, some people write when the kids are in bed," I was advised. (To be fair, this is true—Danielle Steel, for example, famously did this; but Danielle Steel also had seven children, five husbands, and is worth an estimated $600 million. In short, getting by on four hours of sleep a night is only one of many things that Danielle Steel could do that I can almost certainly only aspire to but not, in actuality, pull off.) Suffice to say, my career had started to feel less like something I could be proud of and more like something that I needed to make up for. I needed to be extra good, and breastfeeding was a part of that.

So even when breastfeeding became hell in a recliner, I kept going because I felt like I had no choice. It didn't seem right to take my own feelings into account, and none of the women that I turned to for help suggested that I should. I don't think that these women were cruel, but rather, like me, they'd been conditioned to believe that female suffering doesn't really matter. It's mundane, and just a part of being a woman, so why even bother talking about it, much less trying to fix it? We are experts in self-flagellation, and so when we see a woman beating herself bloody, rather than telling her to stop, we step forward to offer advice on how to better hold the whip. Like, say, pumping eight times a day for *at least* fifteen minutes at a time.

The only reason I eventually stopped trying was because someone else was able to convince me that me being a withering ghost was, like, maybe not so great for the tiny person that was totally dependent on me. This is such a tricky thing to articulate, because of course part of parenting is putting your children's needs before your own, but the point I'm trying to make here is that so often, when women consider our own well-being, we only think of it in terms of how it will benefit others and not how it might benefit us.

We think we should feel good because that is what is best for everyone else, and we've somehow lost the plot because we don't really believe that feeling good is reason enough in itself. When we put on our own mask first, we're doing it in hopes it will help us help others and not because we, like, need to breathe and stuff. I mean, look at her, taking up all that oxygen that could be used by someone else!

It's not uncommon to hear someone jokingly refer to herself as "bad," especially among mothers. However, when pressed for what this woman did that made her bad, it's not like she left her kid in a hot car with the windows up, put whiskey in the baby's bottle, or filled everyone's Christmas stockings with razor blades and firecrackers. Instead, the "bad" thing that she is referring to is usually something along the lines of going out with her friends, letting the kids watch extra TV on a day when she was tired, or eating a cupcake alone in the car because she didn't want to share. All totally normal stuff that made her life, for at least a little bit, easier or more enjoyable for her (I don't know who needs to hear this, but cupcakes are designed to be a *single serving* of cake, and a single serving means the right amount *for one person*). This is the kind of stuff that men do on the daily (I once saw a man at the pool sit down and order himself an IPA and a pizza, then whip out his phone and start scrolling while his wife struggled to put sunscreen on their four kids) without a shred of guilt, yet many women can't do it without feeling like they've failed to fulfill their obligations to others. And lest you forget who we feel obligated to, may I remind you that it is everyone we have ever met and quite a few people we have not.

To stop trying, you have to put yourself first sometimes. You have to stop pushing through pain when you don't have to and start considering yourself when you make decisions. You have to believe, truly believe, that your comfort is as important as anyone else's and that it should not automatically be the first thing on the chopping block when things start to get tough. When you sacrifice yourself, you will do so because it is something you want to do and it was a conscious decision you made. Suffering does not have to be your default, and yet we've been so conditioned to believe that it is that we often feel guilty—which is just another form of suffering—if we're doing anything but.

Most of us would never be so bold as to expect instant gratification in the roles that we play, but our society has taken this to the extreme and taught us to rarely expect any gratification at all. We've gotten used to giving and giving, and then giving some more. However, when we martyr ourselves for others, we often do so because we still believe, deep down, that we'll somehow be rewarded for doing so. And true, maybe we'll be praised for our selflessness, maybe our sacrifice will be recognized (doubtful), but what is almost a zero-possibility outcome is that those who we have always put first will someday do the same for us so that we are able to have and do what we want without having to bear the indignity of asking for it. Eventually, we find ourselves stewing in resentment that makes us feel even guiltier, and now we are suffering for our suffering.

We have to stop letting guilt drive our decisions, and if we can't flat out run it over in the middle of the road, we can at least aim to pack it in the trunk where it belongs. Guilt is a useless emotion, yet we so often base our decisions and choose our plan of action based off what we think will make us feel the least amount of it. This just doesn't work. No one gets to where they want to go—a happy and fulfilled life—by taking whichever roads are paved with the least guilt. Take enough of these roads, though, and you will end up someplace you never wanted to be with no idea how to get back.

When you go your own way, some people in your life will not be happy about this, especially if they're used to their needs coming first. They will find it very inconvenient and might even suggest that you are acting selfishly. When this happens, see if you can remember that when people use the word *selfish*, what they often really mean is that you are no longer doing what works for them. The harsh truth of being a woman is that no matter how much of yourself you give, it will never be enough. So when you give, make sure it is a choice and not a habit, and get in the routine of saving a little piece of yourself for yourself. Do this long enough, and you might even end up with enough pieces to feel whole again.

Much like there will be times in your life when quitting isn't an option and you have to hang in there, there will also be times in your life when you are not able to choose what you sacrifice. There will be plenty of times when forces outside of your control require you to push through pain and suffering. So why not save the pain and suffering for those times? You're not on this planet to play a supporting role in your own life. Your emotional and physical well-being should not be collateral damage. You're not obligated to obliterate yourself for anyone. Not your parents, not your bosses, not your spouse, and not even your children. Gasp, shock, horror! And relief.

# 4

## Maybe You're Not "Just Tired"

So," a friend asked me, taking a sip of her wine, "did you ever think about killing yourself?" We were in a tapas restaurant, and I speared a garlic shrimp, popped it in my mouth, and chewed. We were talking about how, not surprisingly, my spiral down the rabbit hole of trying to breastfeed had eventually led to a severe case of postpartum depression. At the time we were having this conversation, it had been more than four years since I'd crawled out of said hole, and I spoke of PPD often and openly. To friends, to family, in interviews, to therapists, people I just met. And yet, no one had asked me this before. When I swallowed my shrimp and answered honestly, it was the first time I'd said the words out loud.

"No," I said. "But I did think I deserved to die."

Postpartum depression rendered the first six months of my son's life the worst six months of mine, and during that time, I hated myself. I had repeated visions of crossing the street and getting hit by a car. Not a Smartcar or a Prius or even a Honda Accord but a giant truck, like a semi, or a bus, something that would toss my limp body into the air before it crumpled into a pile on the side of the road. On less dire days, I traded this fantasy for a strong punch in the face, a fist, or maybe even a brick—something hard and swift that would knock me out and crush my cheekbones.

I kept these scenes to myself for so long, only telling my friend because she asked so directly, because now I can see them for what they were: the distorted thoughts of someone in the throes of mental illness. But that interpretation has come with time, and perspective, and therapy. When I was experiencing them, though, I had none of that, and these thoughts made perfect sense to me. I felt bad because I was bad. Perfectly reasonable!

In hindsight, of course, I can see that PPD barreled down on me like a runaway train, whistle blaring and lights flashing, but at the time, I didn't see it coming. I was too busy researching power-pumping on a website whose tagline (which made my copywriter's brain howl in protest) was "Breastfeeding—it's too important not to." So even though I cried nonstop, even though I'd curl into a ball on the floor and dig my nails into my palms until the skin broke, I had no idea I was depressed. I thought I was a terrible person—how could I be so ungrateful when I'd just had a baby?!

As first-time parents, my husband and I were laughably naive about the realities of caring for a newborn. When I was eight months pregnant, my husband started a new "dream job," which was a high-level position at a San Francisco–based tech start-up. His previous employer had been incredibly flexible, but this new gig was 100 miles per hour from day one. He was floored with responsibilities and taking weekly trips up to SF that left him exhausted when they were short and me angry when they were long.

My family was far away, and my friends were mostly at work or in a different neighborhood (basically in Los Angeles, far away). I was too embarrassed of my breastfeeding problems to try to meet new people, so I spent most of my days alone with the baby. Occasionally, I'd make plans to get coffee with someone I knew peripherally or had been introduced to, but inevitably, when the morning of or night before rolled around, I'd cancel, simultaneously ashamed of how bad I was doing and overwhelmed by the sheer amount of strategy and planning required to get out of the house. One day, I went outside to get the mail. Standing on the sidewalk with a stack of bills in my hand, I found myself in awe of the cars driving down the street and realized I couldn't remember the last time I'd stepped outside.

Finally, it was my mom who brought it up. "Honey," she said over the phone, "I think you might be depressed." Later that same day, I got a text from a former coworker who had a nine-month-old, asking how things were going. I usually responded to such texts by giving people what I thought they wanted, which was exclamation points and cute baby pics, but this person was different—she was the only person I knew who'd ever talked openly about postpartum depression. "My mom just told me she thinks I'm depressed," I wrote back.

"Sorry to hear that," she responded. "Want to meet for coffee?" I said yes, and this time, I didn't cancel. The following day, I met her at a café, where I got a turmeric latte (tastes like sand in a cup, but everyone knows you're not supposed to have caffeine when you're breastfeeding—or, trying to breastfeed . . .) and we walked around the neighborhood, me pushing my son's stroller while wearing the maxi dress that I wore every day and also slept in, her using one of her precious hours of having a babysitter to listen nonjudgmentally and offer her gentle opinion that it sounded like my mom was right and that what I was describing was more than just your average baby blues.

Shortly thereafter, I started therapy with a woman

who specialized in pre- and postpartum patients, and I slowly started to feel like myself again. Her calm, matter-of-fact approach to PPD made me see it for what it was—a real mental health condition and not the personal failing I had previously interpreted it to be. At the recommendation of a friend, I bought a workbook called *Mind Over Mood* and started to see that some of the patterns that my depression had made seem more appealing—like never leaving the house and avoiding other people—had actually made it worse. I started doing breathing exercises as soon as I got in bed and when I woke up in the middle of the night, and gradually, I started to sleep again. One day, I packed my son into the Ergo, and we set out on a walk. We ambled, stopped for a coffee, sat in the sun for a bit, and I had the strangest feeling—I no longer hated myself. I could even see a lot of ways I was a good mom, even without breastfeeding. That was when it hit me that I probably wasn't depressed anymore.

I continued to see a therapist, though, and to research the topic on my own, and the more I learned about depression, the more I began to see I'd actually struggled with it for much of my life and even had a couple of periods where it deeply affected my day-to-day. Once when I was in middle school and the only thing I looked forward to was sleep. Later, in college, I spent a semester crying as I walked across campus listening to Cat Power on repeat on my red Sony Discman. It never crossed my mind, in those times, that how I felt was anything other than the result of just not being good enough. Maybe if I tried harder to be better then I'd feel better, too. Trying harder usually meant doing more, working harder to make other people happy, and making more of an effort to hide how I was really feeling. Instead of treating myself gently, I layered punishment upon punishment, and doubled down on trying to be perfect. Did this ever make me feel better? Nope! Well, what about worse? Absolutely. Every freaking time, over and over, until my patterns seemed etched in stone.

While I was growing up, I learned that it was shameful to feel anything less than "just fine." What mattered the most was not necessarily how you were doing but how other people thought you were doing. The '80s mentality tended to regard poor mental health as laziness. If you were struggling, it meant that you probably weren't working hard enough to keep it together, and that you were selfish, since even spending enough time thinking about yourself to realize you weren't fine was too much time spent thinking about yourself (since all your time should be spent sacrificing for others, remember?).

I didn't know anyone who went to therapy. I knew one person who took antidepressants, but everyone in her family also took antibiotics every day so they wouldn't "get sick," so she wasn't exactly a positive role model when it came to health care. Mental health issues were treated like the boogery, whiny kid at the playground—if they start to bother you, just try to ignore them until they go away. Don't acknowledge them, don't talk about them, and definitely do not seek help, because what if people found out? What would they think of you then? You can't fix a problem while also pretending that it doesn't exist, so these tactics did little to make anyone feel better.

As I grew up, my environment changed, and social norms changed, and more people began speaking openly about mental health, but I still didn't think this conversation applied to me. For one thing, I thought I had no right to be depressed, since my life was so easy and privileged. What did I have to be depressed about? I just needed to work harder. This is one of depression's cruelest tricks—the more you need help, the less worthy of help you feel. Even at thirty-eight and with a newborn, finally admitting that I was actually depressed felt huge and dramatic, like I was calling attention to myself and becoming a burden to others. Most of all, it felt like a fail, because no matter how hard I had tried to just not feel the way I felt, it hadn't worked. Here I was, someone who was so bad at life that she'd just had a baby and still couldn't manage to be happy. I don't know what exactly I expected from no longer pretending that everything was "fine"—that I would be shunned, judged, or stoned, maybe? That the Bad Mom Police were going to swoop in and take my son away? I was sure that punishment, swift and severe, was coming my way.

The reality, though, was quite the opposite. Being open about my depression didn't push people away. If anything, it pulled them closer, and I was shocked to find that, when we had dismissed with the formalities of pretending everything was great, almost everyone I talked to had experienced something similar at one time or another. I remember once, at a book festival, when I was talking to a group of people I'd just met, I started to cry. I was mortified, as I was a debut author, already feeling intimidated, and immediately began to apologize. "I'm so sorry," I said, "I just had a really hard time after my son's birth . . ."

Before I could get any further, another author—a man!—cut me off. "Hey, don't worry about it," he said, "we're parents. We get it."

Seeking treatment for depression is one of the biggest steps I've ever taken toward accepting myself as I am instead of trying to punish myself into being the person I thought I should be. It has allowed me to understand that sometimes the way I feel is not just because I have not done enough to feel better. Sometimes it's just a glitch in my brain. I don't ever want to go back to where I was mentally after my son was born, and at this point, I'm pretty confident I won't. Does that mean I expect to feel fan-fucking-tastic every day of my life? No, of course not. But it does mean that I now recognize the difference between a dip in emotions due to external circumstances and when my brain is in free-fall mode.

After my first miscarriage, I was incredibly sad, but I still found a lot of joy in my day-to-day life, and the big thing was that I wasn't blaming myself. Me, myself, and I were still a team, and we were getting through it together and we were going to go buy a croissant and then eat it while sitting in the park. A year and a half later, though, after failed fertility treatments, it was a different story. I'd catch the voice in my head saying things like "Of course you can't have another baby. You don't deserve one. You don't even deserve a croissant." After a couple of days of this, I saw that I was starting to hate myself again, which I recognized as a clear sign of depression, so back to therapy I went.

Part of the reason that I struggled with depression for decades before really seeking help is that I was used to struggling and being unhappy. So many symptoms of depression—like excessive tiredness, feeling worthless, incessant guilt, trouble sleeping—also just happen to be the symptoms of being an adult female in the twenty-first century. It's hard to tell where to-be-expected ends and treatable condition begins.

Even women who don't experience clinical depression still find happiness a challenge because, in a lot of ways, it's an extremely difficult time to be alive. We've got young children, aging parents, economic insecurity, shit politics, and periods that might as well have been scripted by Wes Craven himself. If we want a fulfilling life, we're supposed to try to have it all while knowing that we'll probably never get it and even if we do, we might just have to give it all away and oh yeah, no complaining! Honey, don't forget to smile! Also, I hate to say it, but all those towels you washed back in chapter 1? Someone just used them to clean up barbecue sauce. Yeah, all of them. It was a really big spill. And don't forget to smile!

I will never ignore how I feel mentally again, because I firmly believe that decades-long avoidance was one reason why postpartum depression hit me so hard. How I felt was never a priority for me, because I didn't think I was allowed to make it one, and so I just kept shoving emotions down and powering through and hoping that things would get better on their own. They didn't, of course, and I know now that mental health doesn't take care of itself. There's no software update for your brain that just comes in while you're sleeping and fixes all the bugs. You have to actively tend to it, which is tough to do when you're already taking care of so much. If there is only one area of your life where you put yourself first, let it be your own mental health. When you prioritize your emotional and psychological well-being, everything else will be easier, but this is so hard to do because it comes with few external markers of progress and productivity, which means it will often get bumped to the bottom of the list, below school committees and work projects and family reunions or a trillion other things that come with urgency and emails. It's also something that will never be "done." Instead, it must be done over and over—and, yes, this means it's work, and you have enough work to do.

Taking care of your mental health is your foundational work, though, the work that needs to gets done before you do anything else, so what can you quit that will give you the time and space to do it? What are you doing to try to prove—to the world, to yourself—that you're good enough to feel good? Can you ditch that and rededicate that time to something that replenishes you instead of further depletes you? Maybe that is therapy, or reading books, or going to church, or walks in the woods, or journaling. There's no one-size-fits-all prescription, and while others can offer suggestions here, no one can tell you exactly what to do. You have to find out for yourself, and then you have to do it. Even when it feels like doing nothing, or like a luxury you don't possibly have time for, you have to make the time. Or else. But you don't, actually, have to smile.

We tend to think of happiness as a reward, one that is bestowed upon successful people who have earned it. You know, people who are *worthy*. Since we rarely think of ourselves as worthy, it often seems perfectly logical to us that we aren't happy. I mean, who do we think we are to believe that we, too, have a right to be happy?

When we think of happiness as a marker of success, it also becomes competitive, and we start to think that our own happiness is relative to others'. If someone else is happier, then are we really even happy at all? One of the many flaws in this way of thinking is that we don't have any way of reliably gauging someone else's happiness. We're all conditioned to pretend to be doing better than we actually are, yet we tend to take it at face value when other people say they are happy and then compare how we *think* they're doing with how we *know* we're doing. We tell ourselves that we are not happy because we don't have $X$, or haven't accomplished $Y$, so we become harder and harder on ourselves trying to make those things happen. And yet, the harder we are on ourselves in our attempts to be happy, the unhappier we become! You cannot hate and berate yourself into happiness. I know, because I tried it for years and, you guys, it just does not work. At all. Not once. Not ever.

For much of my life, even when I wasn't depressed, genuine happiness eluded me. Sure, I laughed a lot and danced a lot and watched the sun set over the ocean and thought about how lucky I was to be alive. I've had plenty of fleeting moments, but the baseline feeling wasn't there, mostly because I felt I didn't deserve it. I wasn't successful enough to be happy. I thought of happiness as little more than a luxury handbag, like a reward that just had not been bestowed on me because I hadn't earned it yet. I would earn it, I always thought, by chasing achievement, by working hard, by continuing to try even when it felt impossible. All I had to do was thrash myself to stay motivated. Once I was motivated, I'd work really hard, and once I was working really hard, I'd achieve more, and then once I achieved more—ta-fucking-da—I'd be happy because happiness was a goal. Really, it was THE goal, and I knew how to meet goals. You went after them with everything you had.

So, I did just that, for years, and all the while, that ta-da moment stayed just out of reach. Just when I thought I was finally getting close to the finish line and could see happiness on the other side, it would move and I'd find myself suddenly starting a new race before I'd even had time to catch my breath from the first. Okay, so you published your first book? Fine. But was it a bestseller? 'Twas not. Yeah, that's not quite good enough, so your promised happiness is now located further down the road. Pass go, but do not collect $200.

I even took a kind of perverse pride in the fact that I never let myself believe I had anything to be happy about, because I thought it was just more proof of how hardworking and dedicated I was and that I wasn't going to settle for anything less than everything. Why bother being happy now when I could be even happier in the future? That wasn't the road to happiness, it was a dead-end, and all being unhappy really meant was that I was unhappy. It wasn't a badge of honor, it was unfortunate. I was so accustomed to denying myself happiness that even a depression that felt like my soul had been tied to the back of a truck and towed down a dirt road, well, that seemed about right.

We believe that we must try to be happy or try to find happiness because we have been conditioned to believe that happiness exists outside of ourselves. We need some*thing* to make us happy. It's a new car or a new job or a new partner or a new house or more sleep or more children or boobs that produce as much milk as a Guernsey. When we are trying to be happy, we're all trying for something different, but what it all has in common is that it is something we don't have right now and that remains right out of reach. If only we had longer arms, dammit, then we'd definitely be happy!

Happiness isn't a goal. It's not something you can work toward or earn. It's not a reward, something that you do or do not deserve. Being happy isn't about doing everything right or having everything you've ever wanted. While you can't just try to be happy, you can try to do fewer things that make you unhappy, like berating yourself, denying yourself, demanding perfection, and a million other harmful habits that we've adopted as part of trying so hard.

When we talk about happiness, we often tend to think of it not as how we actually experience it but as the fictionalized version we see in the media, and most of these depictions aren't actually depictions of happiness. They're depictions of ecstasy, of people so out of their minds on positive emotions that they run through fields of flowers with their arms spread wide, or take the trouble to first find and purchase a giant ribbon and then tie said giant ribbon around a Kia to gift to their spouse. We think of how it feels when you're falling in love or on vacation someplace with a swim-up bar. We pursue this feeling, and then when it proves either unobtainable or unsustainable, we're even less happy because we feel like we have failed. If you've ever attended a perfectly good party or returned from a really nice vacation, feeling kind of bummed because it wasn't the mind-blowing, life-altering experience you'd been hoping for, then you know exactly what I'm talking about.

I've often thought about how, in all my years of partying (which was, frankly, quite a lot of years), the best nights out were ones that weren't planned. They were when after-work drinks turned into hailing a vintage, white, airbrushed '80s limo to cruise around Manhattan, or when we found ourselves at the club in flip-flops and bike helmets, because why not go dancing on the way home from the beach? On the contrary, nights where we set out to have the best time ever, we inevitably spent all our time in cabs, or waiting for someone to text back, or standing in line, never having fun where we were because what if we could have more fun someplace else? Chasing a high turns everything into a low.

Real-life happiness doesn't require pursuit, nor is it something you get and then keep forever. We have good days and bad days and even bad months, and true happiness comes from rolling with this nonjudgmentally instead of constantly comparing how we actually feel with how we think we should feel. Letting yourself experience the bad days is paramount to letting yourself feel the good ones, too, because if you're in the habit of denying yourself one, then it's inevitable that you'll deny yourself the other.

When you find yourself feeling happy, see if you can break the habit of picking it apart, of parsing out what if any of it you have earned and what must be sent back or delayed until further progress toward perfection has been achieved. Don't reject it because you're holding out for even more. Allowing yourself to experience happiness now does not prevent you from experiencing even greater happiness in the future. Happiness is not a finite thing that can be depleted. There is no need to be cautious. You won't use it up if you gorge on it now. Happiness is unlimited, so go ahead and let it be yours. Do not hold back. Do not try to hoard it. Bathe in happiness. Roll in it. Dance in it. Breathe it in, drink it up, swallow it down. And then, when it seems like it's ready to go, let it. Do not hold on tight and try to force it not to leave. It is not leaving because you didn't try hard enough or are not worthy enough to make it stay. That's just how it goes. One of the big secrets to a happy life is understanding that there's more to life than being happy *all the time*. And isn't that ironic, don't you think?

# 5

## Looking on the Dark Side

My first experience with therapy, in my midtwenties, was a bust. At that point in my life, I was living in New York and working for a fashion magazine. I once divided my salary by hours worked per week and figured out that I would have made more money working for minimum wage. A lot more. I stayed out too late, drank too much, counted a lemon poppy seed muffin from Dean & DeLuca as both breakfast and lunch, and was in a relationship with a guy who once kicked me out of the car and left me on the side of the road in New Jersey.

I knew I needed to fix my life and make better choices, yet, for some reason, every time I went to therapy (which I was paying for out of pocket), the therapist wanted to talk about how my parents had steered me to an in-state university rather than letting me take out loans to go to an expensive, private college (something for which I am actually very grateful!). She was sure I resented this. At one point, I literally said, "I don't think that's my biggest problem right now," and yet, still, that was what we talked about. So, after a few weeks, I decided therapy was not for me ("I'm not thrilled you made this decision on your own," she said; "I barely know you," I responded). It was ten years before PPD prompted my return to therapy, at which point, I discovered that therapy is exactly like dating—it only works with the right person. But in that interim, I found a right-for-now person: a psychic.

I've always been drawn to magic and the supernatural, because it gives me things that I cannot dissect into oblivion. It quells my overthinking, and I need that. Rather than digging into minute details from the past, the psychic just threw things out there. I could accept or reject them, but I couldn't pull them apart. She was like a slightly out-there friend who gave good advice. She once, when I was in a period of extreme overwork, told me I should do as much as I could while lying down, and when I talked to her about how I wasn't happy being single but didn't want to go online, she told me to focus on being open to meeting people in real life. "Don't wear headphones all the time," she said. "And don't always be on your phone or in a book. If

you're standing in line, just look up and look around."
I didn't find love this way, but I did go on a few dates
(with a guy I met on Amtrak and once with someone
from my favorite airport restaurant) without having to
decide on a profile pic.

My psychic and I fell off for a few years in my
midthirties, when my life was rather calm, and then
I reconnected with her when I was trying to get pregnant. I had been on my third cycle of IUI and was
particularly disappointed when this one didn't work
out—even the doctor had been surprised that it
had failed. A few days later, I spoke to her over the
phone and tearfully recounted where we were with
everything. I told her the conclusion I had come to
about why these treatments weren't working for me.
"There's still a part of me that feels like this is never
going to happen," I told her, "and I know that, deep
down, I'm scared of being pregnant and giving birth
again. I was so sick last time, and then the birth was
so hard, and the depression was so rough. I never want
to feel that way again, and I'm worried that I will if I
have another baby. I know I'm supposed to stay positive, and I'm trying so hard, but I just keep failing, and
I know that's why this isn't working."

I told her about how I was doing affirmations—
looking in the mirror, smiling at myself, and saying,
"I am pregnant," about twenty times a day—and visu-

alizations (like imagining myself about to give birth), but that still, the fear was there. I expected her to coach me on new affirmations and new visualizations, and encourage me to keep trusting the universe, but she was quiet for a moment. "Okay," she said, finally. "None of that is true. Your thoughts could be way more negative than they are, and it would still have no bearing on what is happening to you. What you are doing right now is beating yourself up and blaming yourself for something that is not your fault."

I immediately burst into tears. When you are struggling with fertility, few things that people say to you are comforting, but this was. My fears and doubts about pregnancy and childbirth were all very real and valid, yet I was trying so hard to stay positive that I invalidated all of them by considering them all just more of my own flaws.

Much like believing that you should just be able to try to be happy when you're depressed, believing that you should try to stay positive even in the midst of really negative situations just makes things worse. It creates more negativity, because now every time you have a negative thought, it is immediately followed by another negative thought (guilt, shame) over the first negative thought.

Do enough spins in this cycle and, soon, anything even remotely negative (like a realistic assessment of an unfortunate situation) sets the panic alarm, and you're playing mental Whac-A-Mole, the result being that (*whack*) spending so much time trying not to have any negative thoughts or feelings (*whack, whack*) leaves no room for positive ones. Negative emotions are a part of life, and yet we, as a culture, are so uncomfortable with them—especially when experienced by women—that our first instinct is to try to get them to go away as quickly as possible. *Whack-whack-whack-whack-whack!*

The belief that you should stay positive is a form of magical thinking, where we delude ourselves into believing that if we can just keep the bad thoughts from our minds, then we can keep the bad things from our lives. Where it really becomes harmful, though, is when we use it to dismiss pain, be it our own or others'. If you believe that someone's negative experience is the result of their own inability to stay positive, then you do not actually have to do anything or even acknowledge all the factors that have contributed to their pain. If you are the one who has hurt them, then you don't have to acknowledge that, either. Our culture is so militant about positive thinking because it allows us to view societal failures (which we might have to do something about) as personal ones (aka, not our problem!). Someone didn't fail because they were set up to do so, someone failed because they couldn't

stay positive. That's on them, and only them. You get
to blame the victim, look the other way, and feel superior, all in one fell swoop. Believing that success or
defeat hinges on one's ability to stay positive discredits
the very real barriers that can prevent someone from
achieving their goals or even just enjoying their lives
(racism, sexism, ableism, economic inequality, to name
just a few). It's a sandalwood-scented way of gaslight-
ing someone into believing that their thoughts are the
source of all their problems, and creates unnecessary
shame and guilt for a person who probably has a fair
amount of that already.

Women hear a lot about how important it is that
we stay positive, because no one wants to listen to us if
we're not. To actually listen to a woman's complaints—
really, truly hear her out and pay attention—might
make one think that they need to do something about
the negative things she's discussing, or at the very least,
change the narrative that's it's all her fault. And who
wants to do that? It's so much easier to dismiss her
problems as something that's all in her head. So easy,
in fact, that we do it to ourselves. An optimist sees a
glass as half-full, and a pessimist sees it as half-empty.
A woman gets an empty glass and then gets down on
herself for still feeling thirsty.

Difficulties and inequalities and plain old shit sand-
wiches do exist, yet we expend enormous amounts of

energy trying to convince ourselves otherwise. We are
so scared of what will happen if we stop trying to stay
positive that we end up denying our negative emotions
and even our negative experiences. After enough of
this, we end up feeling like we are living a lie and pretending to be someone we're not. We try harder and
harder to feel how we think we should feel, and then
become even more disappointed in ourselves when we
can't. It's natural to not feel totally confident when
you're doing something for the first time, to feel like
an imposter when you advance a level, to be scared
when you're saddling up for your second rodeo after
getting trampled on the first. Experiencing negative
feelings does not mean you're not trying hard enough
to have positive ones. What it does mean is that you're
human.

We feel pressure to force a positive spin on everything because our culture is deeply uncomfortable with
pain. We can't tolerate the discomfort or complexity of
an unhappy ending, because unhappy endings are bad
for business. When people believe that a happy outcome is inevitable if we just keep trying, then we will
of course keep trying! And, once again, when we're
trying, we're spending our money and making other
people money and performing unpaid labor and putting our own needs on the back burner because those
are all things that we have been taught we need to do

to live a good life. And the good lives, we're taught, are the ones where every chapter has a happy ending. That's pure fiction.

The positive thinking paradigm has taught us to believe that every failure has to lead to greater success, every trauma to growth, and that every mistake is a learning experience. If we acknowledge that sometimes things just dead-end at nothing, then we might decide that it's not always worth it to try. And why might we decide that? Because, often, it's not! The reality is that things don't always work out for the best.

Maybe everything does happen for a reason—it's not really possible to label that statement as definitively true or false—but even if it's true, it doesn't diminish pain. And it suggests that even when someone goes through something absolutely awful (abuse, violent crime, extreme loss), it was, on some level, what they needed. When we meet someone's story of loss or disappointment or trauma with "Everything happens for a reason," we are denying them the space to feel what they feel while at the same time blaming them for what they have gone through. It's not comforting, it's condescending and prioritizes our own need to stay in our safe little bubble, where nothing is random and bad things don't really happen, over their need to feel seen and heard.

You don't have to make everything that has happened to you into a positive. When we tell our stories, we should be able to say, "It sucks," instead of "It sucks, but . . ." because we know that's what our audience wants to hear. We are not always going to fail up. Sometimes we will fail and fall down the stairs. When this happens, we shouldn't have to hide our bruises because we are worried they are going to give someone else the ick. We're so well trained to value other people's emotions more than our own that we feel obligated to spin our stories into something that makes other people feel good no matter how bad we actually feel. "Well, everyone I've ever loved just burned up in a fire," we say. "But it's not that bad, because I'm really able to focus on myself now. The house burned down, too, and I lost everything I've ever owned, but hey, guess I don't have a kitchen to clean anymore. So, yeah, um, what shows are *you* watching these days?"

We can also unwittingly force others into this position as well. A lot of us are conditioned to feel like when we see someone struggling, we should try to make them feel better because we have been taught that everyone else's emotions are our responsibility. We're expected to be caregivers. We're accustomed to people coming to us because they expect us to fix their problems, and just listening can feel like doing nothing. We find ourselves telling them to look on the bright side or reminding them that it's not all bad, because at least that feels like something. But nothing is often exactly what people need.

Validating someone's negative feelings, instead of implying that they haven't tried hard enough to solve the problem, or that it's all going to turn out for the best, is more helpful than anything else you can do. When I told people about my miscarriages and my decision to stop trying for another baby, I didn't need to be reminded that children were so expensive anyway or that siblings fight all the time, or of how lucky I was to already have my son. I didn't need someone else to tell me he was a miracle. (Trust me, I know.) What I did need was someone to listen and let me know that it was okay that I was hurting.

"No regrets" is yet another shaming phrase disguised as philosophy. Yes, maybe it's not that great to beat yourself up about the things you regret, but know what else isn't great? Beating yourself up for having regrets because you feel like you shouldn't have them at all. I have plenty of regrets—I regret not freezing my eggs, I regret that my husband and I didn't start trying for children as soon as we knew that was what we wanted together—and simply allowing myself to feel those regrets is not the same as obsessing over how things might have been or dwelling. It's okay to occasionally wonder how things might have been different for you if you had done something differently. Experiencing regret is a natural consequence of the fact that you're not a robot, that you acknowledge your autonomy, and that you're thinking about the big picture of your life. These are all good things, and they don't need to be swept under the rug just because they're not catchy ideas that fit easily onto the side of a water bottle.

It's no surprise that existing in a culture that deemphasizes negativity to the point of denial leaves us phenomenally unprepared to experience grief. After three miscarriages, I had dealt with a fair amount of grief about the pregnancies I had lost, but that was nothing compared to the grief that came with the settling realization that all the expectations I had, all the visions, all the planning for another baby, were also lost. I could stop filing away names that I liked because there would be no one to name. I could give away all the baby clothes I'd been saving because there would be no one to wear them.

I was sad and mad, and at first, I saw my grief as a problem that needed to be fixed. Like, what *the fuck* am I going to do about this sadness? I'd rant and rail about it to my therapist, about how unfair it all was (*Send it back! This is not what I ordered!*) and at first, it frustrated me that she didn't offer me any solutions. All she would say was "That is worth mourning." Finally, I started to see what she meant. There was no way around the sadness. Grief is like a bear hunt: can't go over it, can't go under it, gotta go through it.

This means sharing it, airing it out before it starts to stink, not hiding it, packing it away in that little box, along with the old prom corsages and *Phantom of the Opera* playbill, that we only ever open when we're home alone and have had our one glass of wine. This means making people uncomfortable. This means dropping conversational bombs and then sitting in the aftermath, the awkward silence as whoever you're talking to begins to realize that the story you've told is done and it's not a fairy tale. No one gets to go through life without losing something, without having something ripped from you before you were ready to let it go, even if that's "just" a dream. Grief comes for us all, and so for god's sake, let the people have their grief! Let yourself have it, too. We could all move through our grief and negativity so much easier, and probably faster, if we just let ourselves experience it instead of trying so hard to pretend that it's not there because we've been told that's the right thing to do.

There is no such thing as unjustified grief, but we often act like there is because we find ourselves experiencing it even when we got what we wanted or are going through something that we have chosen. Every time you make a choice, you are leaving something behind, you are telling something no, and there's a certain sadness to that. You can choose to move to a new city and still grieve the city that you left behind, for example, and get a little emo when you think about how your life might have been if you had stayed. These are probably the kind of negative feelings where it's not fruitful to spend too much time with them, but you're still not doing yourself any favors if you deny them completely. This was something that came up for me a lot when I chose to stop trying to have another baby. Yes, I chose to move on. Yes, it was my decision. But sometimes you make a decision not because you want to but because you have to, and so it still hurts like hell to make.

This kind of grief denial is especially true when we're talking about anything related to motherhood and children, topics that often engender a militancy about staying positive. I had a very hard time as a new mother, and I know a lot of other people who did as well, and so often, a part of what made things so hard was that we were hit totally by surprise. "Nobody told me there'd be days like this," she says, not singing along to John Lennon but bouncing on an exercise ball for the ninth hour straight. This is a direct consequence of the culture of toxic positivity that surrounds motherhood. Women continually find themselves in the dark, completely unprepared, because we live in a culture that is more concerned with pretending the dark side doesn't exist than it was making sure everyone is prepared with candles and a flashlight. Why did Chrissy Teigen's Twitter teach me more about postpartum depression than any doctor or birth educator ever did?

At the time I was going through postpartum depression, I was spending most of my time sitting in a chair with either a surgical tube taped to my boob, or attached to a concrete-block-sized breast pump that plugged into the wall because that was the one that was supposed to be "the best." I didn't have a lot of mobility, or free hands, so the activities I could participate in were fairly limited. All it takes to scroll Instagram, though, is a fingertip, and so that's what I did, even though it was about the worst thing I could do. At the time, several of my friends were also new mothers, and each time I came across one of their pictures, it felt like a punch in the face. There they were, serenely cuddled up with their baby, or breastfeeding in a corner booth at a chic restaurant, or just generally being so happy and competent in their new motherhood that it would have made me cry if I wasn't crying already.

I remember one friend who posted that she was going to take some time off social media so that she could really enjoy this blissful, cozy time at home with her newborn. I liked her post and then hit Mute, immediately berating myself for not being happier for her and for not being able to say the same. I wasn't nesting, I was panicking and frantically ordering garbage from Amazon in the hopes that maybe the next package drop-kicked to my door might be the one that would solve all my problems. Cozy, it was not. A few days later, this same friend texted me to say she hadn't stopped crying since she got home from the hospital and had never felt worse in her life.

Even when motherhood is something that you have dreamed of for years, even when it is something that you want with every cell in your body, and even when it goes exactly as you planned, there is still grief. Why? Because your life will never be the same. The specifics are fuzzy now, but I remember once, shortly after my son was born, listening to a podcast where a woman talked about how she'd realized, the first time she left her baby with a babysitter, that being a mother meant that she'd never be alone with her thoughts again. That hit hard because it was so succinct and well put. You will never again be able to only consider yourself, your life will never again just be about you, and I think the fact that this isn't something that is ever really talked about or acknowledged shows how little respect our society holds for the lives of women without children.

A baby is a bomb that detonates life as you knew it, and I say this as someone who wanted a second bomb more than almost anything in the world. We have to give women the room to mourn the fact that their life just got blown the fuck up, that in many cases, their body just got blown the fuck up, too, without giving them a patronizing smile and reminding them, "Yes, but wasn't it all worth it?" Because they're not saying it wasn't worth it. They're simply saying that the fall-out hurts, and there's a difference there. Big difference. You'd be hard-pressed to find a single experience in life that is not, at least in some way, a mix of the good and the bad, and being honest about this is not a sign of ingratitude for the experience in the first place.

One of the many casualties of the obsession with positive spin is that it convinces us that "good" experiences are the only ones we can be proud of. But experience is experience. It all makes you who you are, and sometimes—though not always—it makes you into a better person. I don't know if I'm a better person after these last few years, but I know for a fact I'm a different person. You don't always get back up the same way after you've been knocked down, but that's not something to be ashamed of or hide. When we learn to be proud of our negative experiences, then we're one step closer to being proud of the person that we are instead of believing that pride is only reserved for the person we thought we should be.

Failing, getting hurt, having your ass handed to you on a Heath Ceramics platter—do you know what all of that is proof of? All of it is proof that you tried. And trying, ultimately, is a good thing because when you try at something, it means you care, and none of us want to go through life without caring about anything because that wouldn't be much of a life at all. In spite of its title, this book is not about how to stop trying at anything ever again. It is just about how you can stop trying when you really don't give a shit so that you can continue to try when you do.

You do not have to try to stay positive in the face of disappointment. You are allowed all of your emotions. You are allowed to be sad, to be frustrated, to be pissed off. You are allowed your rage, your regrets, and your grief. You are even—wait for it, wait for it—allowed to be bitter. Yep, that B-word, which dismisses all negativity and dissatisfaction a person has as merely their own inability to *get over it already*. *Bitter* is a death sentence for women, because once we label a woman as *bitter*, then we do not have to listen to a single word she has to say.

So, I'll say it before anyone else does, and with my apologies to Jill Sobule, but I am bitter as fuck these days. I can look around and see that this reckoning I'm experiencing right now, and that so many women I know are also experiencing, is not all our fault. I can see that the reality of trying to have it all is really just doing it all. I can see many areas of my life, from the time I was a little girl right up until pretty much this morning, where I have been denied the support I needed. I can see individual people and institutions who taught me to devalue myself because it served them better, and others who straight up didn't care about me at all. I can see so many instances where I was punished for not knowing things that no one ever bothered to teach me, and other times where I tried my hardest only to be told that it wasn't quite hard enough. If I pretend that I am not bitter, in the name of staying positive, then I am doing a favor to bad faith and broken systems, but not to myself. Or to you— because I bet you've got a little bit of bitterness in you, too. If you say, "Oh no, no, no, not me, I don't have a bitter bone in my body," then may I remind you, yet once again, of the towels . . .

Someday, I will move on from all of this. Someday, I will forgive everyone and everything that has hurt me. Someday, I will be positive, not because I'm trying to stay that way but because that is how I actually feel. But today is not that day, and that is okay! So if you're with me, let's sit around and be bitter old bitches together. I have a highly disappointing nonalcoholic aperitif that I ordered off an Instagram ad, and I am more than happy to share. It's quite bitter, too.

# 6

## Closure Is a Myth

In my twenties, I worked as a beauty editor at a women's magazine. The salary was low, but the perks were high, as publicists were always cooking up different ways—like a designer bag or a fancy luncheon—to bring attention to new products. This is how I came to receive a free astrology reading, and though I cannot at all remember what product this was supposed to promote, I do remember the reading.

I provided my time and place of birth, and a few weeks later, an astrologer named Matthew arrived at my office, wearing a long black trench coat and black beret—not exactly the gauzy scarves and gemstone jewelry I had been expecting. As we shuffled into a windowless conference room, I was unsure what my co-workers thought I was doing, but Matthew's reading—

which he was thoughtful enough to record on tape for me—proceeded to blow my mind. It was my first real experience with astrology, outside of newspaper horoscopes, and I was in disbelief as he ripped through aspects of my life and personality like he had known me forever. One thing in particular stood out to me: "Don't get married before you're twenty-nine. If you get married before you're twenty-nine, you'll just get divorced."

"Got it!" I said. "Thanks for letting me know!" I was twenty-three, freshly graduated from college and new to New York, where dating felt both exhilarating and impossible. I'd always imagined myself getting married and having kids someday, so hearing the advice that I should be careful *not* to do so for the next six years was oddly freeing. After all, I was a person who was constantly planning for and worrying about the future, but this made it seem like I could relax a bit and have fun. I dated and had a few relationships, including with a guy I started to date seriously a few years later.

The first red flag, suggesting this one was not exactly marriage material, began waving when he bought me a forty-gallon freshwater aquarium for my birthday. I had never wanted so much as one goldfish, but he'd long been obsessed with the fact that he didn't have room for an aquarium in his own apartment and frequently suggested that I, with my largish bedroom in Greenpoint, could easily take on some fish. "But I don't want an aquarium," I had repeated, over and over, in no uncertain terms. Yet on my birthday, there it was, in my bedroom, along with several puddles, wet towels, and the IKEA dresser that he'd conned my roommate into helping him hastily assemble because I didn't own any furniture that could accommodate an approximately 450-pound glass rectangle of water.

The aquarium was a disaster. For one thing, I immediately recognized that there was no way an IKEA dresser—co-built by a chef and a writer—could hold 450 pounds of glass and water, so the aquarium had to be drained and moved to the floor. Then I got renter's insurance because I wasn't totally convinced that the floor of my apartment could hold that much additional weight, either. I didn't want to be the girl who was forever in the poorhouse because she'd dripped water and guppies into the neighbor's bedroom below and was still paying off the damages.

The problems weren't solved once the aquarium was on the floor. The water soon turned brown, and it became infested with snails. The fish ate one another. It was very hard to get the pH right, and I had to constantly add different chemicals—sixty-two drops of this, seventeen drops of that—to keep the fish that weren't getting eaten from suffocating. To change the water, I had to carry full buckets back and forth to the bathtub, sloshing all the way through the apartment as my roommates sat on the couch, smoking weed out of a modified highlighter and having a good laugh at my misfortune. The only thing that kept me from having a full-on meltdown about it was pretending that the aquarium was just the comedic subplot in a sitcom, complete with laugh track every time I spilled on my shoes.

Whenever I mentioned that I wasn't exactly enjoying having an aquarium, the boyfriend would remind me how much it had cost (so, so much money). Finally, I worked up the courage to drain the aquarium for good, got rid of the boyfriend, and found myself single at twenty-nine. Twenty-nine, the age that Matthew had prophesied all those years before. That meant it was time to get serious.

I carefully selected the first guy I dated after that. He was in his early thirties, owned his own business, condo, and even had a dog. *Ding, ding, ding!* I thought. *We have a winner.* This guy was marriage material. Except, almost right off the bat, nothing went how I thought it would. He was late a lot. He'd cancel plans when other things came up. I came back from being out of town for a week and he made no effort to see me. We texted a bit, me always dropping hints about how *great it was to be back from vacation*, but still no effort on his part to see me. Finally, I'd had it—he was clearly over it, but I wanted to make sure that he knew that I knew he was over it and therefore so was I. So, one night, about a week after I got back, I sent him an email. This is the dating equivalent of hearing a sound in the basement and going down into the dark to investigate—don't do it! If you know what is best for you, do not do it!

But I did it. I didn't want this situationship to fade into a nothingship. I wanted to give him the opportunity to make it right or, at the very least, I wanted closure. I edited those two paragraphs for hours until they were perfect, and then I hit Send. Almost immediately, he wrote back, which is never a good sign. And it wasn't. "You're cool and I enjoyed hanging out with you," he said, "but you aren't a priority, because I'm not in love with you." If having a door slammed in your face counts as closure, I guess I got closure.

Still, I didn't learn my lesson. I started dating someone else, and as soon as it seemed like maybe we weren't headed into long-term-relationship territory, I went to my keyboard and started drafting. This guy, unfortunately, was someone I liked a lot, and so I wanted him to know that it was all or nothing: he could either be my boyfriend, or we couldn't hang out at all, not even as friends. This last part was going to be hard, because we had started out as such and shared several close friends, but I was determined to define what we were, even if that definition turned out to be nothing. When he wrote back a couple of days later, I ran to my bedroom and shut the door to read the email. All he'd written was "Got it, I understand." I saw him that very night, when we found ourselves at the same bar, with the same group of people. Bartender—one shot of awkward, please, and make it the kind that burns going down.

*Closure* is one of those words, like *boundaries*, that has become so ubiquitous in our culture that it has lost much of its meaning. It's not uncommon to hear people say things like "It really violates my boundaries when you act like yourself, so could you please stop doing it?" or "I set fire to her garage because *I* needed to do what *I* needed to do to get closure." Wait, what? However, long before it became diluted therapy speak, *closure* was used to describe a cognitive feat: when we looked at something that was unfinished, like a circle missing part of the line, the brain still viewed it as complete. But now, when we talk about closure, we usually use the word to mean an event or a certain knowledge that makes us feel better about a previously unfinished situation. This might look like obtaining a final bit of missing information, having a chance to get something off your chest, or receiving a much-needed apology before moving on. Regardless of the specifics, when we talk about closure, we usually imagine it coming from something, or someone, outside of ourselves. It's almost like we see ourselves as an incomplete circle in need of its missing piece before it's ready to roll.

We place so much importance on getting closure because it implies the presence of finality, a locked door that will never open again, but that's rarely how life works. There is no magic key that will hide something away so that it never bothers you or surfaces again. Nine times out of ten, when we refer to *closure*, we're talking about a negative situation, or a situation that was negative for us. There's often a power imbalance in the need for closure, too, in that those who are powerless are seeking closure from those who are in power, and it is rarely the other way around—people rarely seek closure from the person they have ghosted or from an employee they've just fired. So, when we do find ourselves in the position of the powerless, we imagine that closure will make a painful situation hurt less or make a complicated, confusing situation more straightforward.

Once we have closure, we can say, "Honestly, I'm so over it," and actually, ya know, mean it. Sometimes, surely, closure does work this way, but more often than not, by seeking closure, we are keeping ourselves stuck. Trying to find closure in a situation can keep you locked in that very situation and prevent you from rolling on, because now you're looking at the person, or thing, or experience that hurt you so much and asking that very same thing to make the hurt better. You are looking to what made you feel incomplete in the first place and now asking it to make you whole.

Seeking closure rarely goes how you imagine it in your head and often leaves you feeling even more disempowered than you felt before you sought it. Those email responses from guys I liked didn't make me feel better—they made me feel worse. And I don't know anyone who has ever requested an exit interview and had it go as hoped. No, instead someone from HR listens politely to your laundry list of complaints, then lets you know you still need to clean out your desk and asks if you've received a packet detailing the end date of your health insurance.

Sometimes, we think that closure will not come from another person but from a sign that proves we were on the right path all along. When this is the case, we're usually not actually seeking closure but instead looking for a reason why we shouldn't move on just yet. We want something to convince us that something isn't as over as it seems and give us a reason to keep the door open and stay right where we are. After my final miscarriage, my doctor offered to do another battery of tests. Most of them I'd had before, and I got the sense that she was offering because she wanted to offer me *something*, not because she thought we would learn anything new. I got as far as sitting in the lab in that little chair with the arm pillow, my veins splayed out for the phlebotomist, before I decided that I'd save myself some trouble—and blood. Even if the tests did reveal something we didn't already know, what was I going to do with that information? Actually, I knew exactly what I would do with that information: use it to beat myself up with shouldas, couldas, and wouldas; imagining the outcome if I'd had it years ago; and using it as a reason to embark on a new round of even more tests and procedures. And that was the best-case scenario. Most likely, the test results would only reinforce what I already knew, which was that sometimes infertility and pregnancy loss just happen.

Often, even if we know deep down why something didn't work out, we still seek closure from an outside source because we don't trust ourselves. We intuitively know a lot more than we give ourselves credit for, but we live in a world that has conditioned us to feel that we are almost always in the wrong and therefore must depend on outside confirmation to know if we're correct. We learn, over time, not to listen to the little voice inside that tells us when something feels right or not. When I was a teenager, things seemed to go south for me—as in the cops calling my mom at work to have her come pick me up kind of south—never when I was having a blast, but on nights when I was already uncomfortable and someplace I didn't want to be with people I wasn't sure I liked. Instead of asking someone to drop me at home or voicing my thoughts that none of us should be doing what we were about to do, I would tell myself to chill out, to not be so uptight, to stop worrying because no one else was—*Oh, hello, Officer, how can we help you?*

When we hear the phrase *women's intuition*, we often roll our eyes. We have come to think of it as akin to saying that we believe we're psychic, and we would rather write something off as coincidence than give our intuition credit for it. Yet, if we take a step back and look at the big picture, our lives are positively lousy with coincidences. Think of all the times your eyes have popped open in the middle of the night, and you're lying there in bed for a couple of minutes before you hear a little voice call out, "Mommy, I don't feel good . . ." Or when you've sent a text out of the blue to a friend you haven't heard from in a while, and they respond immediately with "I was just thinking about you!" Or turned on the radio to hear the song that was just running through your head. Sure, it could be a coincidence that you experience so many coincidences. Or not.

Part of the reason that we have such a hard time listening to our own intuition is that we have been taught, our entire lives, to listen to other people. Listening to other people is a huge part of being an obedient child, and few qualities are prized in children (especially girls) as much as the tendency to do what one is told. The downside of this is that we often carry this with us for the rest of our lives, and we're constantly looking outward, to other people and things, to tell us how to feel and what to do, and there's no shortage of sources willing to do so. Instead, there's a surplus, and the more external voices you hear, the harder time you will have listening to your own.

I still have moments of downright panic when I start to think that maybe I've been mistaken this whole time and that I need to call the fertility clinic right now and do whatever it takes to have another child, but those moments usually come after I've been scrolling through social media or have read another pregnancy announcement from a celebrity well into her forties. In my soul, I know we did what was best for our family, but when I pay too much attention to the noise, the doubt grows and I start to panic—*What if I've gotten it all wrong!?!* I've also learned the hard way that private browsers aren't only for nefarious web surfing—sometimes they are just for private browsing. One google of "fertility after 40" was all it took to be barraged with ads for everything from fertility tests to egg donors and online courses, all of which offered a cure for my ills—at a price, of course. Never before have we been exposed to so much information that has been tailored and customized just for us, though we have to remind ourselves that this is not really for our benefit. It's for those who have something to sell us and who are likely to profit off our pain. Sure, sometimes that pain is only the desire for a cute pair of pajamas, and in that case, serve 'em up, Instagram, because I am happy to be influenced! But when it comes to big life decisions, the ones that are highly personal, I don't need to be the target customer in someone's marketing strategy.

When making decisions, we often map out the pros and cons, but how we *feel* rarely makes it onto those lists because it seems too ephemeral and, we tell ourselves, inconsequential. In my ten years of running my own writing business, I've learned that my very first impression of a client, and whether or not they would be a pain or a pleasure to work with, often proved correct. Sometimes I didn't vibe with someone on the initial call, but I took the job anyway because the pay was good or because I thought it would look good on my résumé, only to discover that it wasn't worth it because the client didn't respect my time, was (as Gen Z would say) completely delulu, or had no intention of giving me what I needed to do the job and do it well.

Sometimes, it's not the external voices that are the hardest to ignore but the internal ones, especially if you have a tendency toward anxiety or intrusive thoughts. But if you look closely at those intrusive or anxious thoughts, most of them will reveal themselves to be external in origin, even if you've been repeating them for years. Someone, at some point, started you on the path to second-guessing yourself, and so you've been doing it ever since.

When I was growing up, I lived right near a river that basically ran from my house to my best friend's house. We were in that river nonstop (which is how I once got hit in the head with a live carp), catching everything we could in our little net, from turtles and frogs and crawfish to, once, a goldfish, and then canoeing as teenagers, a pastime that inevitably involved at least one capsize and left everyone soaking wet. I told that story once, not too long ago, and the person I was talking to looked at me in horror. "You didn't worry about snakes?" he said, totally aghast. No, I had never worried about snakes, but you can bet I worry about snakes every time I walk along the riverbank now.

Unlike intrusive thoughts or anxiety, intuition is rarely fear-based. True, when we think of it, we might think of a plane crash and someone saying they'd bought a ticket but something told them not to take the ride, but that doesn't happen very often, and when it does, it is usually in the movies. Instead, intuition usually comes with a sense of optimism and calm, whereas an intrusive thought is all about disaster and catastrophe. Intuitive thoughts make you feel good, whereas intrusive thoughts invite panic. Intuition is patient and often presents solutions to problems, whereas intrusive thoughts create more of them and demand action right now.

For example, whenever I'd have a call with a potential client and something just seemed off, my intrusive thoughts would come in strong, freaking out that maybe this was going to be the only job opportunity that I was going to get, that maybe I was going to run out of money if I didn't say yes, that maybe my career would be over if I didn't take that one job. Intuition, on the other hand, would tell me that a better fit would come along soon, and it almost always did.

Culturally, we have a hard time with intuition because from the outside, it often seems illogical and we place a high value on logic. Intuition is hard to explain to other people, and as a result, we can end up facing pushback on some of our most intuitive decisions. That's a hard pill to swallow if you've been taught to place a high value on others' approval or to always listen to the "experts." We are material girls living in a material world, and we often believe that everything in our lives can and should be measured by something external. To shift your focus internally, and listen to yourself above anyone else, requires swimming upstream. There are plenty of forces in your life, in all our lives, who would prefer that you kept going with the flow until you're right where everyone else wants you to be. These aren't always sinister forces. Sometimes, they could just be a concerned friend or family member who thinks you're about to make a mistake or who feels slightly hurt that you're not trying to make your life look more like theirs. In these cases, as hard as it may be, you have to remind yourself that you don't owe anyone explanations, nor are you ever required to share.

Often, we feel a strong desire to overexplain our own decisions because we're trying to get everyone on our page, to see where we're coming from, and sure, you can do this if you want to, but you don't have to. You, you adult human female you, are allowed to make your own decisions. You do not need permission to do so. You can move on whenever you are ready. You don't have to seek closure. You can create it instead.

Nevertheless, it can be hard to really feel like you have closure when, from the outside, everything looks just the same as it ever was. This is where ritual comes in, which actually has a lot in common with intuition because it's another thing that we've kind of lost reverence for. Our modern lives are devoid of ritual, and once you've hit those big milestones—graduations, marriages, anything where you wear a certain type of gown and take a long walk while people watch you—it can be hard to delineate between one phase of your life and another. This is especially true as you get older and grand gestures—like a solo trek through South America to solidify a newfound sense of independence— aren't always possible.

But small rituals, done with reverence, can serve the same purpose and can signify your intent to end one chapter so that you may begin another. For a long time, I kept a memory box of my fertility struggles, where I tucked away talismans like positive pregnancy tests, a rock from the beach I'd visited after learning I'd had a miscarriage, a blue jay feather found on a hike, that sort of thing. Closure for me meant getting rid of it all, as well as the cursed ovulation monitor that had, for three years, dictated my outlook on life. The pregnancy tests and monitor were plastic, so I wrapped those separately, in a piece of cloth that had once belonged to my husband's mother, and everything else, the nature bits, I tucked in a small straw basket, along with some blood I'd saved from my last miscarriage, as something in me had recoiled against the thought of flushing all my final pregnancy down the toilet.

On a warm spring day, I took these things to a small lake where I often go for walks. It is surrounded by woods filled with creeks and meandering paths, and my son and I have had storybook days there, filled with turtles and hopping frogs, and tossing seeds and leaves into the water. After I discarded the plastic stuff in the trash, I placed everything in the basket into the lake and then sat down and talked to myself, out loud, for a while. I told myself all those things that my intuition had been telling me for months, that my life was still beautiful, that I was still worthy, and that my family and I were going to be fine. When I'd finally talked myself out, I got up and finished my walk, then drove home feeling pretty much the same as I'd felt on the drive there.

I understand that there is no magic closure that is going to make it easy to move on from this part of my life. This ritual didn't make the hurt go away or suddenly bless me with divine understanding. What it did do, though, was signify that I was moving on even though I knew it was going to be hard. It represented a newfound belief that I knew what was best for me and that I didn't have to wait for a door to slam in my face. I could get up and gently close it myself.

# 7

---

# Over Achieving

I left full-time work to go out on my own in 2014, right when millennial grind culture was at peak frenzy, and I remember feeling a distinct sense of pride that I could identify with so many memes and LinkedIn posts. Yeah, girl, I know what it's like to come home from work and do more work! Lemme just go ahead and hit Like on that and then I'll #hashtag my #hashtags and swing by this networking event (if I'm not too busy working!) and there is no way in pale pink hell I am ordering a latte and NOT posting a pic of it and OMG, do I need more coffee because I am very sleep deprived but must keep working because I buy my own health insurance now and that is $$$$!

This period of my life was the apex of my work ethic and ambition, the result of a drive I'd been honing since my freshman year of high school. I remember heading into ninth grade with a clear desire to be popular (not unusual, given the steady diet of teen movies and magazines I consumed) and a feeling that it was really, really important that people liked me. I knew that being "involved" was key to social acceptance/ dominance, so the summer before school started, I signed up for the tennis team. I was actually pretty good at tennis, had a lot of fun at practice, and, to my shock, I wound up with a decent position on the junior varsity team and an upperclassman for a doubles partner. Score one—er, fifteen?—for Kate.

Come fall, I decided to join the yearbook staff. Once again, nothing about it was contrived—I love writing and photography, and especially loved the "press pass" that allowed me to roam the halls and interview people I wanted to get to know. Not too bad for a freshman who had spent much of her summer worrying that someone was going to pelt her with raw eggs and mustard as she walked into school on her first day (thank you, *Dazed and Confused*)! All in all, I was pretty proud of myself.

Then one afternoon, I found myself in conversation with a sophomore boy. I casually shared that I was playing tennis and had joined the yearbook staff. I'm not sure what I expected—that maybe he would be impressed?—but instead he responded, "Oh, that's it?"

I was floored. It wasn't like this guy did a lot; I remember him as being a baseball player who smoked a lot of weed and worked at a cell phone store. But maybe that was precisely it. If even a slacker thought I was slacking, then clearly I had some work to do.

From that day forward, I made sure that no one else would ever fail to be impressed by my extracurricular engagement, and I joined every team, committee, club, and council that would have me. By the time I graduated from high school, my "résumé" was three pages long.

In college, I continued much the same. I wrote for the school newspaper, literary magazine, and alumni journal. I went on volunteer trips and did PR for a nonprofit. I won school-wide and national awards for my writing. After one unfortunate C in Econ 101 summer school (the same summer my roommate's boyfriend decided to perfect his pot brownie recipe), I doubled down on my grades and pulled down a 4.0 my entire junior and senior year. I also worked a part-time job waiting tables at a brunch restaurant, which meant regularly waking up in a panic at 6:20 and then speeding across town (it was a small town) to arrive by 6:40 for my 6:30 shift.

By the time my college graduation rolled around, I was already long gone—because I'd gotten a job at a magazine and moved to New York. To this day, the only proof I have that I graduated from college is a paperweight, because I was too busy to ever pick up my diploma. "It's just a piece of paper," I explained and didn't care at all, because college was already in the rearview, receding faster and faster as my career took off. I was promoted at the magazine I worked for, then got a job at a different magazine, then another. I wrote cover stories and flew around the world and lunched with celebrities like it was no big deal.

Then, in my late twenties, I traded my magazine job for one in brand marketing and, with it, traded small budgets for big ones. I got a corporate card with a limit that was more than my salary. I got promoted and promoted and promoted. In my "spare" time, I freelanced, blogged, took writing classes, worked on my novel, and traveled, frequently going out of town for two or more weekends a month.

When I went full-time freelance, I had a twelve-year corporate career behind me, and I couldn't wait to be boss-free and manage my own schedule. Maybe I'd sleep late or go party on a Tuesday! Instead, I chose to exercise my total control over my own time by working seven days a week. I'd wake up in the morning, make myself a cup of coffee, and then head downstairs to my desk, where I'd sit until the middle of the afternoon, when I'd suddenly realize I was still in my pajamas, hadn't brushed my teeth, and hadn't even finished my coffee, much less eaten breakfast or lunch, because I was too busy working.

After my son was born, I scaled back to working part-time, but still managed to publish four books under my own name and ghostwrite another in the first five years of his life. When people would ask what my writing process was, I would joke, "Panic," the joke being, of course, that it wasn't really a joke. Overachieving was my humblebrag, and I told myself that I just liked being someone who got a lot done and had a full plate. Sure, I regularly found myself nearly immobilized by how much I had to do, but I always figured that was no big deal, a small price to pay for the validation I got for working so hard and doing so much. And if I kept my head down and stayed that way, then I didn't have to admit the truth: I got a lot done, but just barely. And that full plate? It was cracked.

Scraping it all into the trash—or, at least, some of it—never seemed like an option, though, because I had built my whole identity around being an overachiever. Even though I constantly struggled, I figured this was how I always had been and always would be. That was just how it was for me. It wasn't until I found myself short on reading material one morning, in a doctor's office waiting room, that I began to think otherwise.

As I sat waiting for my appointment, I picked up

a book about ADHD and began to flip through it. Though I was familiar with ADHD, I had never really read about it. A few pages into this book, my jaw dropped, because I might as well have been reading my life story. Over the next few days, I devoured the rest of the book, my head spinning. This was the first time that I had ever heard that there is a high correlation between workaholism and ADHD, and that ADHD is often underdiagnosed in girls and women because we tend to present very differently than boys and men. We're less likely to be hyperactive or impulsive. Instead, women with ADHD often struggle with tuning out. We procrastinate and can't stay organized, and then we—wait for it, wait for it—often overachieve to mask it.

I was always a dreamy and out-of-it child. My family members called me a *space cadet* because it was so hard to get me to pay attention to whatever was going on around me. In elementary school, I remember being entirely flummoxed by worksheets like word searches or crossword puzzles, math problems that required me to show my work, or anything that necessitated following step-by-step, precise instructions. I could knock a diorama or book report out of the park, but I couldn't find *PIZZA* in that field of letters to save my life. By junior high, my teachers often reported that I spent most of my time in class staring out the window. How much so is illustrated for me, now, thirty years later, in the fact that I have few clear memories of schoolwork, yet I can recall, as detailed and clear as if I were looking at a picture, an American flag that flapped above the treetops outside of the window of my third-floor math class.

I lived in a perpetual state of disorganization. No matter how many cute pink locker organizers I installed in September, by October, my locker was a black hole where assignments and school supplies went to die. At home, my room looked like it was time to call in FEMA, with a foot-high, wall-to-wall layer of stuff on the floor. When I was old enough to drive and got a 1987 Honda Accord to call my very own, I kept it in a similar state—that apple core fermenting in a Taco Bell cup isn't trash, it's science!—and I coasted most places with a gas tank on E, buying only two or three dollars of gas at a time.

It often seemed like I worked harder than everyone around me not because I necessarily wanted to but because that was just what it took. I needed to be high-functioning to function at all. This was nothing I could articulate, though, or even really put my finger on. All I knew was that I almost always felt less than, so I doubled down by doing more because I'd figured out that people tended to overlook that you were struggling with the minimum when you were able to deliver on the maximum. Sure, I got to class late and then often slept right through it, but then I was also captain of the tennis team, editor in chief of the yearbook, class president, prom queen, and worked a part-time job. I had plenty of reasons to be late. And to be tired.

When it came to academics, procrastination was the name of my game. I saved everything until the last minute, even though I started to fret and worry about schoolwork as soon as it was assigned. In college, with no parental supervision, I regularly pulled all-nighters, printing out my due-at-8:00-a.m. essays on my dot matrix as the sun came up.

Once I landed a job at a magazine after college, I applied these same frantic, last-minute tendencies to my work. My desk always looked like a dump, covered with old coffee cups, piles of papers, and various other things that had come to die in the graveyard that was my workspace. My inbox filled with unanswered emails and my voicemail with unreturned calls, and yet I was constantly taking on more and more work. I volunteered for every story I could, did extra work for other departments, went out of my way to help anyone who needed it, and did freelance on the side. Often, I'd wake up in a panic and start responding to emails at 4:00 a.m., only to fall back asleep at 6:00 and, of course, end up being late for work. Even when I was an entry-level, brand-new employee, I was late, so I made up for it by staying even later and coming in on the weekends.

The more I climbed the ladder, the later I got. On my last day at work in Philadelphia, at a job I'd had for five years and truly, truly loved, I left my apartment to go to work at 10:30. Work started at 9:00, but who cared? I'd already quit! But then, somehow on the freeway, driving a route that I drove twice a day, I got in the wrong lane and soon found myself heading the opposite direction from where I needed to go. I wound up on the bridge going across the river into New Jersey, a bridge that required a cash toll to get back into the city. I, of course, didn't have any cash and was about to run out of gas, so once I got to Camden, I first had to drive around to find a gas station and then a working ATM, before finally getting back on my normal route to the office. By the time I got to work, it was already past noon. I found out that my creative director had sent out a company-wide email about my leaving, and all morning, people had been coming by to congratulate me only to find an empty chair.

Reading about ADHD made all this make sense in a way it never had before, and I soon went to a specialist for an official evaluation and diagnosis. I then brought my diagnosis back to the doctor whose waiting room had given me access to the ADHD book in the first place. "So, what does this information empower you to do?" he asked.

We sat in silence for a bit as I contemplated this.

"Hell if I know," I said finally. But over the next few days and weeks, I continued to think about it, and the same thought kept bubbling up to the surface. The first four decades of my life had always felt slightly out of control. I had lived in a fugue state of stress and overwhelm, constantly playing catch-up, and was always tired because I always felt like I had to do twice as much as the next person just to be on their level. Learning that I had ADHD helped me to understand why this was and helped me to see that being an over-achiever was not who I was. Rather, it was both a defensive mechanism and coping strategy. So what this information empowered me to do was change and stop trying to do so goddamn much all the time.

For a lot of overachievers, we somewhere, somehow, learned that love was something that would not be given—it had to be earned. So we set out to earn it. We worked. When our work wins us accolades and praise and recognition, well, that feels like love, and we begin to believe that it's not who we are that makes us lovable, but what we do. So we keep doing it, because who wants to be unloved?

For my entire academic and professional life, work was everything to me because it was the one area where I felt competent. The external validation I received from it was important because it counteracted the lack of validation I gave myself. I was so often focused on all the things I was doing wrong that it was really nice to hear that somebody—anybody? anybody?—thought I was doing something right. The idea of deliberately turning my back on one of the main things that had always earned me approval was terrifying, but not nearly as much as the thought of someday burning out beyond repair, a thought that was seeming less and less like a possibility and more and more like an inevitability with every passing day.

For some people, high achievement comes naturally, and they barely break a sweat. I once worked for a woman who lived in LA, commuted to New York, ran an art gallery, was raising two teenage boys, and yet would still offer to dog sit if she heard you were going out of town. She was unflappable. She thrived on having a packed schedule and lots of responsibilities, and truly enjoyed doing things for other people. Overachievers are different. We're flappable and sweaty. Rather than doing so much because it's truly no big deal, because we find it fun, or because we relish the challenge, we pile it on because we're scared of what will happen or how we will be seen if we don't. We often think of ourselves as naturally lazy, or incompetent, or undeserving, or all three (because we're overachievers, of course!). Over-delivering helps us convince ourselves that we're not and is also a nice little "look at the birdie" that keeps others focused on the areas of our lives that we want them to see so that we can continue to hide the ones that we don't. We're not trying to succeed as much as we're trying not to fail. No amount of achievement will ever make us feel truly secure.

Often, it's our very fear of failure that sets us up for it; we develop impossible expectations for ourselves that we then fail to meet because it is literally impossible to do so, and then double down on ourselves in a misguided attempt to make up for it. We're perfectionists, too, so even when we do manage to pull off those impossible feats, we're rarely satisfied with ourselves and instead tend to focus on what went wrong and obsess over how we're going to do better next time. It's an exhausting and unfulfilling way to live, but you probably don't need me to tell you that.

When I knew I was ready to put this twenty-five-year "phase" behind me, I started by making small changes to my day-to-day patterns, and also really examining how those patterns had formed in the first place. Two of the biggest things that had always bugged me about myself and that helped convince me that I was unworthy were that I was generally messy and frequently late. What both of these usually stemmed from was the belief that I needed to pack in as much as I possibly could or else risk falling behind. I didn't have, I thought, the two minutes it would take to put the sandwich stuff back in the fridge or go through the papers on my desk, because I needed to allocate those two minutes to making progress on one more task. Same with being late—the map said it would take fifteen minutes to get there, but I could respond to one more email if I tried to make it in twelve. Awareness is so often the antidote, and so on days when I was tempted to leave the kitchen looking like the dog had just gone counter surfing, I'd pause and remind myself, *You have plenty of time to put away the pickles.* It was a big light bulb moment when I realized that some of the things I liked least about myself had persisted for so long because I literally did not believe I deserved the time it would take to change them.

I also started to evaluate all my responsibilities and my opportunities to take on more by looking at each individually: Yes, I could do that, but did I want to? And if I did want to, why? Was it because it was something that I would enjoy, or that would add value to my and my family's life, or did I want to do it because I wanted to be known for doing it, because I was scared I wasn't doing enough already? I liked the idea of being in charge of all the social media for my son's school because then it would be clear to everyone that I wasn't slacking on my volunteer hours, but did I really want to be taking the pictures and writing the captions and answering questions on Facebook? Um, no, not at all, not one teeny-tiny bit.

I also started to set boundaries around the work I did take on, something I'd previously never done because I feared it made me look lazy or that I was trying to skate by on the bare minimum. I'd done my fair share of Sunday-morning meetings and 9:00 p.m. calls, but no more. To my surprise, no one was turned off by this. On the contrary, one client later told me that part of the reason she'd hired me was because I'd laid out my available hours in our very first call, and rather than interpreting it as an unwillingness to work, she thought it made me look professional.

It's still hard, though, to wean myself off overachieving because, in so many ways, overachieving is the norm these days. It often feels like this is what is expected of us and just what it takes to get by, especially when it comes to motherhood. Our mothers served up Hamburger Helper for dinner and washed their faces with bars of soap they bought at the grocery store. We're peeling and steaming and pulverizing organic carrots to make muffins and doing ten-step skincare routines using products that we specially ordered from three different websites. "I feel like I'm doing so much," one of the busiest and most health-conscious women I know told me once in confidence, "but I'm not baking my own bread."

We are exposed to a nonstop barrage of details of other people's lives, and no matter how much we are doing, everyone else seems to be doing more. Even if you're an overachiever at work, you're a slacker if you don't apply that same manic work ethic to your family. And your home. And to your self-care. And your relationships. To everything, really, because once you've glimpsed that someone else is able to achieve perfection, it seems remiss to not at least try to do the same for yourself.

Social media has presented us with opportunities that we have never had before, one of which is the ability to gain status and get paid for doing things that have traditionally been completely overlooked and undervalued in our society—basically, "women's work." People who do this are called *influencers*, a term that I am sure you have never once heard in your entire life, and not four bajillion times a day, every day, for the last decade.

On a theoretical level, influencer culture sounds amazing, because now you can see women who have become hyper-successful and who are making megabucks because they're so good at cooking, or cleaning, or putting together an outfit, or crafting, or momming, or exercising, or healthy eating. On a practical level, though, it's a different story, and influencer culture isn't so amazing, because it makes us all feel like crap. It exposes us to a constant drip of perfection since we're seeing the output of people who are profiting from showing us the area of their life in which they are exceptional and convincing us that we can be that exceptional in that area, too. We see white kitchens, poreless skin, seventeen-ingredient superfood smoothies, "daily" Pilates routines, flower-dyed onesies, business milestones, fridgescaping (seriously, wtf?), and Greek vacations, all from different sources, yet coming together to form the whole of what looks like a complete picture of a good life.

Even though we might, deep down, know that this is a false picture—and that making that smoothie is only possible if you don't have to leave the house until noon—a part of us also wants to believe what we see. Maybe these pictures are proof that perfection is possible, and all we need to do is try a little bit harder and set that alarm clock a few minutes earlier. Oh, and keep our own imperfectness, and brown cabinets, under wraps.

What we don't see, and what takes superhuman strength to never forget (even for a few moments), is that no one's life is perfect, no one is perfect. Often, when we're able to step back and observe a bit, we can see that most people are pretty forgiving of imperfection and that much of the time, the super-high expectations that we're trying to meet are our own. I remember once driving all over town and spending a whole week gathering the materials to make a toddler sensory bin that I had seen in a momfluencer's post. When it was finally finished, I presented it to my son, who futzed with it for maybe a minute before going back to playing with a stick he found in the driveway. I used to try to come up with all these ideas to make better school lunches, making Pinterest boards and then staying up late to cook cute little egg cups or assemble turkey pinwheels, and then inevitably, they'd come home from school the next day totally untouched. No person that I actually knew had suggested to me that I do these things, they were just my own interpretation of what it took to meet the expectations of being a good mom.

Sometimes, we overachieve because we want to prove that we can do hard things. So we do a hard thing, and another hard thing, and then soon enough, all we're doing is hard things, and we've forgotten that we can do easy ones, too. Hard things are not the only ones worth doing, and on many occasions, it is the easy things we do that will bring us the most joy, the most satisfaction, the deepest sense of belonging. We don't ever want to take it easy, though, because we fear that this means we are slacking and just as undeserving as we secretly suspect. You are allowed to take the easy way, occasionally, all the time, or whenever you damn well choose. Instead of reprimanding yourself for taking a shortcut, remind yourself that you are merely following a "desire path," letting your heart lead you down the shortest, easiest, least treacherous route to get where you want to go.

Overachieving so often starts with a desire to prove yourself, but then it just keeps going, and going, and going, until it's the bulk of our identity. Who are we? Overachievers! What do we want? More work to do! But wait, wait, wait—that's not really what we want. What we want is to be seen and to feel like we have value. We want to feel loved, and it is possible to have that without working ourselves to the bone. This isn't an easy transition, especially if overachieving feels like all you've ever known. Where do we go, if not above and beyond? Will anyone still want us in the group if we're not doing 98 percent of the project? What are we even doing if we're not making people think, *I don't know how she does it*? What we're doing is letting go of a survival strategy that is threatening our survival. We're learning that not doing everything does not mean that we're doing nothing.

Forming an identity in the first place is a tricky thing. Letting that identity go so that you can embrace a new one is trickier, and trickier still is integrating who you once were with who you are now. We so often treat our identities as if they were set in stone and as if they were something that was assigned to us. We didn't get to pick, but someone came along and handed us a grab bag of characteristics and labels and said, "Here, this is you," and now we're stuck carrying around *bad driver / late sleeper / workaholic / hosts Thanksgiving dinner* until we die. This isn't true. You do not have to be who other people think you are. You don't even have to be who you think you are. We can change who we are, we can become the person that we want to be, a person who feels much more at ease with herself, at any time in our lives. You do not have to keep doing so much just because that is what you have always done.

We often suss out the person other people want us to be by seeing what gets us praised and what gets us criticized. We became overachievers because we saw that saying, "Here, I can do that," made the people around us happy, so we started saying it more, playing up the accommodating, never-complaining side of ourselves. Saying "That's too much" or "I don't want to do that" made people unhappy, so we started saying it less and worked to hide the fact that we were tired or stressed out. We are always working, and working hard, because we think that's the price we must pay just to exist.

It is going to take work to do less work, but if there is anything that I know about you, it's that you're not scared of a little bit of work. You eat little bits of work for breakfast (literally, when you make a seventeen-ingredient smoothie). When you make the decision to stop overachieving, you'll probably realize that there are areas of your life where you do still want to exceed expectations, and hopefully you'll have more time and space and energy to do just that, when you're not feeling like you have to do that with every little thing that comes your way. Overachieve because you want to, not because you're scared of who you'll be if you don't.

Overachieving doesn't have to just be a defense. It can be a superpower, carefully deployed at just the right moment. When we're traveling somewhere new and my husband notices I've got a furrowed brow and haven't looked up from my phone for the last thirty minutes, he knows to leave me alone. I'm probably cross-referencing TripAdvisor, Yelp, and a blog post from 2017 to find us someplace to go to dinner. When my extra-mile effort lands us at a Louisiana bayou bar, full on crab legs and dancing the Cupid Shuffle with a bunch of eighty-year-olds, I will be the first to admit that I'm an overachiever and damn proud of it. I put in the work not because I was scared I'd disappoint everyone if I pointed to the Subway across the parking lot and suggested we go there. I put in the work because I wanted to have fun!

When we finally pull our nose away from the grindstone, not only can we start to breathe, we can also see that overachievers are quite magical. We throw amazing parties, put together mind-blowing presentations, give incredible gifts. We go above and beyond and do things that no one thought could be done, and it's time we gave ourselves credit for that. Fuck yes, we can knock it out of the park when we want to. But we don't *have* to. That's the thing—we don't have to.

We are worthy even if we show up empty-handed, if we do the bare minimum, if we don't do anything at all, if the map of our lives is nothing but desire paths, we are still good enough to get where we want to go. We are good enough, even, to enjoy where we are right now, and good enough to rest.

In a yoga class I attend regularly, the teacher is always encouraging us to opt out of the vinyasa, to chill in child's pose or go straight to downward dog, skipping the chaturangas. For a long time, I never listened to him and never skipped the vinyasa. Even when my arms were trembling at the end of class, I pushed through the push-ups, because I wasn't someone who came to yoga just to lie on the floor. But one morning, he got my attention. "Skip the vinyasa if you need to. If you want to!" he called out. "Do not be an overachiever." I found myself dropping to child's pose automatically, because I could finally see that it was okay for me to take the break that I both wanted and needed. We are still hard workers, even if we don't work hard all the time.

# 8

## I Believe in a Thing Called Luck

When my fourth novel, a young adult thriller called *Never Coming Home*, came out a couple of years ago, it was the best thing I'd ever written. As a woman, I know that I'm not supposed to say I made something that was good. I'm supposed to feign humility, downplay my strengths, and wait for someone else to sing my praises, lest I—egad, the horrors!—come across as thinking too much of myself. But I'm going to say it anyway: *Never Coming Home* was a really good book. It still is.

The first draft that I wrote was okay, but on the second draft, I knocked it out of the park. "Kate," my editor wrote back, "this is AMAZING!" That's the kind of editorial feedback that you always want, and this time, I actually got it. I'd written a book where what ended up on the page matched what I'd envisioned in my head. I'd also emotionally poured myself into it. Through the pandemic and three miscarriages, I worked on my own self-hatred by giving it to my characters and letting them hash it out on paper. We learned to forgive ourselves together, and I grew to love them, flaws and all, and was genuinely sorry when—spoiler alert!—I had to kill them off.

In my typical overachiever fashion, I poured myself into marketing it. I hired a Gen Z assistant to help me identify the right #booktok and #bookstagram accounts, then spent thousands of dollars making custom-printed sleep masks and fake hotel key chains, which I then packed up in custom-printed boxes, complete with seashells and sand and gummy palm trees (which I personally packaged, while wearing plastic gloves so as not to touch anything that someone was going to eat, and tied with shiny metallic twist ties) to really drive home the beach theme. I made so many trips to the post office that the employees started to recognize me and let me cut the line.

I also did Twitter takeovers, wrote a guest article, filmed IG stories, reposted mentions, ran paid ads on social media, and spoke on podcasts. I set up online events, and in-person events, and an in-person launch, for which I bought lots of beach-themed décor to try to turn the bookstore into a tropical island (the post office employees did not attend, even though they were invited). Then, I anxiously watched the performance of the book that I was sure was going to turn me into a bestselling author. And . . . crickets.

The book didn't become a #booktok sensation. None of the influencers I'd sent gummy palm trees to made videos declaring me their new favorite author. It didn't hit any bestseller lists. My social media following didn't balloon. It barely blipped. Within a couple of weeks, the online chatter had died down. In many ways, it felt like the book I'd spent three years working on, the book I'd poured myself into, had never even come out at all.

And yet . . . I wasn't crushed. I wasn't telling myself that I was a shit author and that the book was bad, because I knew that wasn't true. Nor was I telling myself that I hadn't tried hard enough, because I knew that wasn't true, either. I was a good author who had tried really hard, and it just hadn't worked out like I had wanted. Not for any particular reason, but just because sometimes that's how it goes.

This is when I knew I'd changed. Rather than dwelling and beating myself up about an outcome that was less dazzling than I'd desired, I was able to shrug and move on because I finally understood, on a deeper level, that success, or the lack thereof, wasn't all about me. Whether things did or did not work out had little to do with what I "deserved," and a lot to do with luck.

You can probably see why it's beneficial to admit that our mistakes and failures aren't entirely within our control, because it means we don't have to beat ourselves up so much about them, nor do we have to regard each and every one as proof of our inherent unworthiness. So why is this still so hard to do? Because if we're going to believe that the bad stuff that happens to us isn't always entirely in our control, then it stands to reason that the good stuff that happens to us is equally uncontrollable. For most of us, this is a deal-breaker, and it can especially be so for women who have been taught that we must work for every little thing we get. We've all seen how often a woman's success is written off with "She got lucky" when she's actually worked her butt off, and we don't want that to be said about us.

But in every success story, luck plays a role, even if it's just a no-name extra that makes it on-screen for a split second and never speaks a word. I owe my entire career to being in the right place at the right time. In college, my last graduation requirement was a two-week internship. Through an alumnus, I was offered one at a magazine in New York, which I almost turned down. I'd never been to New York before, and I wasn't sure if I could afford to stay in the city that long. But once I arrived, I was hooked. I didn't want to go home. "Maybe they'll offer you a job," my friend suggested on a Friday night as I mourned the fact that my internship was already half over.

"There's no way they're going to offer me a job," I said, taking a sip of my PBR, the only drink one could afford on an intern's salary (and even then, you often had to smuggle it into the bar in your purse). And yet somehow, on Monday, that was exactly what happened.

The previous week, the top editor's assistant had lost a check—apparently the last straw in a string of costly mishaps—and been fired. As soon as she was done cleaning out her desk, I moved into it and started answering the editor's phone (this was 2003, so people still had landlines), opening her mail, managing her calendar, and doing other assistant-type things. And *boom*, I became the assistant.

Part of my job was to open and file all the résumés we got from people looking for jobs (again, this was 2003, so people sent résumés on paper). After a couple of weeks, I started to notice something familiar about the résumés that I was filing. Everyone who was seeking an entry-level magazine position had a college degree, a good GPA, lots of writing clips, work experience, volunteer experience, internship experience, tons of extracurriculars, had won awards, and had even studied abroad. Overachievers all, just like I was.

If I'd tried to get my job by sending in my résumé, I would have gone right into the file cabinet with everyone else. What had gotten me the job was that I was already there, warming up the seat. Sure, I had worked to get the internship in the first place. I had been cheerful and pleasant to work with and had done a good job. But I could have been all of these things and still never gotten the job. What I had that those other people in the filing cabinet didn't was a butt in a chair. Aka, luck.

Acknowledging the substantial influence of chance in our lives doesn't mean that you should stop working for what you want or that you should start seeing everyone else's success as unwarranted. What it does mean is that you should give yourself a little more space from both your successes and your failures. This is so, so hard to do, though, when we've been taught our whole lives that it's the exact opposite. We've been raised to believe that *everything* is our fault, and so we'd better try extra hard to control it all—*or else!* It can be a huge weight off your shoulders to observe what you have and have not been able to accomplish with some perspective. No matter what situation you are in, there is only so much you can do. On one hand, this is terrifying: You can do absolutely everything right all the time and still not get what you want. On the other hand, it's freeing: You don't have to worry so much about getting everything right all the time. You can let go a little bit and know that this doesn't mean that you're losing your grip.

Everything that you have in your life is a mix of the choices you made and the forces outside of your control. As André 3000 said, "You can plan a pretty picnic, but you can't predict the weather." That's why it's so dangerous when we tell ourselves, "If she can do it, I can, too!" Sometimes that might be true, but most of the time you can replicate someone's playbook move for move and not get the same results. Because her success isn't just about what she did but where and when she did it, who was there, who wasn't there, which way the wind was blowing, whether or not Mercury was in retrograde, if the L train was running, if someone else used the last Nespresso pod, if there was a wreck on the 405, what celebrity debuted her new bangs that day, which presidential candidate tweeted something egregious (we know which one), whether the moon was full, and literally everything else in the universe. Look to other people for inspiration as much as you want; just remember that what you're looking at is a rough sketch for success (drawn by a three-year-old with a highlighter and an eyebrow pencil), not a blueprint.

For years, so much of my trying was driven by the idea of what I thought I did and didn't deserve. Trying made me good, and if I was good, then I deserved good things. Good things were a reward for my goodness, which meant that I then also saw all bad things as punishment for my badness. If I tried hard enough, then maybe I could be good enough to permanently avoid anything bad or even just slightly disappointing. In all of this thinking, I ignored one of the biggest truisms of life, which is that shit happens, and all the trying, all the goodness in the world, is not enough to prevent it from someday happening to you.

Most of us don't 100 percent "deserve" anything, good or bad, that happens to us, yet it's a word that we throw around all the time because it helps us, at least on the surface, make sense of the unexplainable. We want to believe that life is fair and that all booms and busts are distributed accordingly, rather than admitting that you're not in total control of what you get.

The times we are living in are uncertain—they always have been and always will be—and life is a lot more unpredictable than we would care to acknowledge. When something bad happens to us, or when we don't get what we want, blaming ourselves can actually be a form of self-soothing. If it's our fault, then we can modify ourselves and our behavior and prevent anything like this from ever happening again.

Overachievers especially tend to discount what's out of our control because we want to believe that there is no problem that can't be solved, or even prevented in the first place, with hundreds of hours of relentless hard work. Surely risk can be eliminated if we just try hard enough! Success isn't just about work, though. It's also about chance, and the horrible truth of life is that you can be the best damn contestant that *Wheel of Fortune* has ever seen and still hit bankrupt on every spin.

Perfectionism is, unfortunately, in a very toxic long-term relationship with catastrophic thinking, and they go everywhere toegether. We find ourselves believing that everything is riding on every detail and that if we don't get every detail as perfect as it can possibly be, then it is all going to fall apart and it is all going to be our fault! Whether or not something does or does not work out rarely comes down to one thing, though. If we're the right person for the job, then we're going to get it even if the margins were slightly off on one slide of the pitch deck. If we don't get the job, then there were probably other factors aside from that half-centimeter difference in white space on the left side of page 13 of our résumé. I'll pause here for a second, because even the thought of such an oversight might have you squirming with discomfort. Deep breaths, people, deep breaths.

You're human, and you are allowed to make mistakes. You are also allowed to fail. Hitting bankrupt once does not mean you'll never again have the chance to buy a vowel. Sometimes things in your life will not work out, no matter how hard you try, no matter how much you want them to, no matter how much of yourself you pour into what you are doing. When this happens, the ensuing grief and disappointment you'll experience are punishment enough. You don't have to punish yourself on top of it by telling yourself that the reason you didn't get the outcome you wanted is because you aren't good enough to deserve it.

We are pretty used to things moving at a breakneck pace, and we believe that speeding forward is the only way to get anywhere. With this mindset, it's easy to see why we often interpret failure as hitting a wall rather than just another bump in the road, and mistakes as detours that mean we'll never reach our destination. I'm not suggesting that making mistakes and experiencing failure is enjoyable, but it does bring an opportunity to vary our pace a little bit. Mistakes often make us pause, reflect on where we've been and where we want to go before we hit the gas again. Failure can be a signal that it is time to reassess. It can bring about something that we don't get nearly enough—a break. We all need a flop era every once in a while because it gives us a chance to lie down. You'll get back up, you won't stay prostrate forever, so just try to flop somewhere nice and soft and get some rest.

So many of us are kind and understanding when other people make mistakes, yet we can't forgive our own. We keep a mental list of every time we've ever screwed up or not been able to make something work out and then use that list as thirteen reasons or thirty-seven reasons or eighty-two reasons why we should keep denying ourselves rest, satisfaction, compassion, joy, or whatever it is we so desperately need but don't think we deserve. You have two choices here: You can decide you deserve it all, the good and the bad, right now, and start allowing yourself everything. Or you can decide you don't deserve any of it, never have, and let yourself off the hook for all those things you've always blamed yourself for. Whatever you pick, you've moved forward, because now you either think you deserve the good or didn't deserve the bad, and either way, you're on the path to someday blending the two together and believing both. This isn't about not taking responsibility for your own actions or never admitting when you were in the wrong. It's about not trying to control every little thing in your life and then beating yourself up when it turns out that you can't.

For years, I told myself I wasn't able to sustain a pregnancy because I was too old, had smoked too many Marlboro Lights in the '90s, had spent my fertile years yearning after a guy who washed his dishes in the bathtub because his house didn't have a sink. I pored over my past choices and decisions to find reasons why what I now wanted was something I did not deserve. But then, I kept watching women older than I was, who'd smoked a lot more than just Marlboro Lights, have babies with no problem. It wasn't because they deserved it and I didn't. It was just because, when it came to fertility, I got a bad roll of the dice. That's my luck, not my fault. To quote Dire Straits, a band I discovered on the *Empire Records* soundtrack, sometimes you're the windshield, sometimes you're the bug. That's just how it goes. So, when you're the bug, know that it's not just because you didn't try hard enough to be the windshield. There's nothing you could have done. And when you're the windshield, know there's nothing you could have done about that, either. Life is a highway, so allow yourself to crank the radio and enjoy the drive.

# 9

## No Worries

Throughout my twenties and thirties, I was plagued with diarrhea. Not actual diarrhea, mind you, but the fear of it. I'd go days, weeks, without thinking about it, and then as soon as something important came up, as soon as I found myself someplace where a bathroom was not readily available, I'd start to worry that maybe, right now, even though I felt totally fine, something was festering deep within my intestines and was going to explode any minute.

These fears would pop up when I was working. What if I'm in the middle of a celebrity interview and have to excuse myself, not just for one minute but for twenty? Or I'm supposed to go on a hike with Hilary Duff! Will she still answer my questions about her divorce after I've had to stop and poop in the woods?

On airplanes, the fear would come back, in force, the second the plane pulled away from the jet bridge. This particular worry of mine was so persistent that it became well known among the people closest to me. "Don't go anywhere without Pepto-Bismol," my roommate advised. Others tried to help me devise a plan of action. My sister and I were traveling in Thailand when we met a cute American guy staying at our hotel, and when he revealed that he was a commercial airline pilot, my sister squealed and punched me in the arm. "Oh my god, this is your chance!" she said. "Ask him!" Now, mind you, I was single at the time. Very single. And this was a cute guy, with a good job, who liked to travel. So, I did hesitate for a second.

But when he looked at me quizzically and said, "Ask me what?" I decided to go for it. This was more important than my love life. Deep breath. "I just want to know," I said, "like, what are you supposed to do if you have to go to the bathroom when the fasten seat belt sign is on? Like, what if you get food poisoning or something? I know you're not supposed to leave your seat, but . . ." The look on his face made me trail off, because he was looking at me like I was absolutely nuts, but then he seemed to get that I was serious.

"Okay," he said. "Just go. Make a run for it. The flight attendants will understand." These words brought even more relief than the Pepto-Bismol.

I hadn't come to this crippling fear of bowel mutiny out of nowhere, though, because I was plagued with stomach problems that made it seem like a very real possibility. Almost as soon as I graduated from college and moved to New York, I started to have pains and bouts of nausea that left me distracted and paranoid, excusing myself from dinners and conversations to take deep breaths in the bathroom or pace on the sidewalk while trying not to puke. The fact that these episodes never once actually ended in barfing did nothing to quell my fear, and I never drew the connection that my stomach often started to hurt just when I started to worry about my stomach hurting. But just because it had never happened before didn't mean it couldn't happen now!

In fact, that previous sentence pretty much summed up my view on life, because I approached everything, from major events to the most minor of details, dragging a giant bag of what-ifs right along with me. What if I was late? What if I died? What if I went broke? What if that headache was a brain tumor, that fatigue cancer? What if I got fired? What if I embarrassed myself? What if no one ever called me back ever again?

Basically, I worried. A lot. I often bemoaned my fate and considered myself supremely unlucky, because I noticed a pattern where I'd get one worry eradicated only to have another one pop up to take its place. Even good things—like getting an assignment for a cover story or going on a trip—were just more reasons to worry. There were so many ways a good thing could go wrong! It was so frustrating. Not to mention, so, so exhausting! I often felt sorry for myself, like I'd gotten a bad roll of the dice. How wretched was I, to be given so many things to worry about, so many burdens to bear, doomed to nary a day of carefree existence.

At the same time, I needed my worry, because being a worrier helped me show the world that I was the person it wanted me to be. When I was highly attuned to the danger that lurked around each corner, it was proof that I was responsible. When I was worried about what could go wrong, and double- and triple-checked everything I did for mistakes or overlooked details, it showed how hard I worked. When I got a good opportunity and immediately started to worry about how it might go bad, I showed that I knew I didn't actually deserve it, and when I worried about whether or not other people were happy, or comfortable, or getting everything they wanted at that particular moment in time, it showed how much I cared about others and how little I cared about myself. Responsible, hardworking, self-sacrificing, and suspicious of fun—pretty much your textbook definition of a good girl.

On the surface, this sounds kind of nuts, like I

thought I was responsible for everything and everyone. But at the same time, I bet you kind of know what I'm writing about here and that some of these thoughts and feelings resonate with you, because in so many ways, women of our generation were raised to believe we were responsible for, if not everything, at least everyone. We were raised to be people-pleasers, and we learned early on how to modify ourselves to make others happy. We learned how to sublimate our own needs and anticipate everyone else's because that was how we kept the peace, and emotional caregiving habits die hard. If we felt like it was our job to keep other people happy, that's because it often literally was.

Worrying often goes hand in hand with people-pleasing, because when you're a people-pleaser, you are constantly worried about someone—anyone, anywhere—being displeased. I have spent much of my life doing things that I didn't want to do, or not doing things that I did, because that is what I thought I needed to do to keep the people around me—be they friends, family, or coworkers—happy. If I was asked to do something, I often did not feel like saying no was an option, and since this was how I felt, I made the assumption that this was how other people felt as well. I was always terrified of putting someone else in that position, so I tried to never ask for anything. I figured that if I asked, someone would feel like they had to say yes, even if they didn't want to, and so then they would resent me and see me as a burden. Becoming burdensome was, I figured, the fast track to a life of loneliness.

This was one of the things I worried about the most, starting in my teens and persisting up through my thirties; I always worried that I was just a hair away from causing everyone I wanted to care about me to decide that I was *just too much* and therefore not worth it. I wrongly saw relationships as transactional and thought that the surest way to end one was to require more from someone else than they were getting from me. I worried that anything less than total self-sufficiency was sure to wear people out and drive them away. I remember once, when my car broke down in the days before Uber, walking three miles home with a basket of clean laundry because I thought it was "too much" to call someone to come pick me up.

I worried that anything that went wrong, anywhere, could and would be blamed on me. I'd feel terribly guilty if I was out to eat with someone and they didn't like the food or their order came out wrong. If I was the one who suggested this restaurant in the first place, then forget it—I should just find the nearest veterinarian and ask to be put down. On a rational level, I knew I didn't work at the restaurant and therefore was not allowed in the kitchen, but deep down, I felt like it was an oversight on my part to not have done more to prevent the person I was with from having to endure the horrors of biting into an overdone burger. If I suggested a book or movie to someone and they came back and told me they didn't like it, then I felt bad that I did and that I didn't do a better job of anticipating their tastes while keeping mine copacetic. On my own, I could take a traffic jam in stride, but if there were other people in the car, I started to panic, sure that they blamed me for the bumper-to-bumper because I was the one who suggested going somewhere in the first place. I knew I deserved the blame, too, and all of their ill will, because only someone as awful as I was would want to leave the house.

That, right there, was really the germ of it, the seed of commonality inside every worry I ever had. The reason I worried so much about bad things happening was because I didn't like myself all that much, and so I thought that bad was what I deserved. And while I'm sure most men I know easily attributed an overdone burger or a traffic jam to forces outside his control—and perhaps even blamed those forces!—for me, that simply wasn't an option. All I could see was my personal responsibility and my personal abject failure in everything.

When we are young and tender, we rely on the world

to tell us who we are, and if it is telling us we are bad, then that is what we will believe. If we are shown that each mistake we make reveals yet another flaw in our character, we will become terrified of anything going wrong because it will reveal new ways in which we ourselves are also wrong. As much as worry makes us miserable, it is also our shield, our way of trying to protect the fragile sense of self we have managed to construct. If something bad happens, it might tear away a chunk of our identity, maybe even one of the chunks that we like or are proud of. Who are you to think you're responsible? Would a responsible person have let *this* happen?

Worry is a form of self-punishment that keeps us from enjoying anything good that happens, and that keeps everything we really want—relaxation, joy, or a sense of accomplishment—just out of reach. It keeps us locked in a cycle of trying, too, convinced that if we could just try harder next time, then maybe we'll get it right. How will we know that we've finally gotten it right? When we don't have to worry about it anymore! Except we will never reach that point.

When we believe that worry is our job and that worry is an integral part of how we prove our worth, then no matter how much we worry, it will never be enough. Nowhere, I would argue, is this felt as intensely as it is in motherhood, where the worries are so vivid and so real that they make the fear of pooping your pants on an airplane seem like NBD. Being a mother in the age of pandemics and climate change and political nightmares and social media makes you feel like the world is on your shoulders, with so many ways to carry it wrong and so few ways to handle it right. No matter how much you worry, and no matter how much that worry prompts you to do, you will almost always feel guilty because you feel like maybe you haven't quite worried enough.

Moms are often mocked for our tendency to worry and our inability to relax, but should something go wrong, we'll be punished for not having done enough to prevent it. In families and relationships, who worries about things and who does not is often drawn along gender lines, as illustrated by meme statements like "Behind every stressed woman is a man who's not worried about it at all." These men will often proclaim that they don't need to worry, because things always work out for them, either willfully ignoring or just ignorant of the fact that things often work out because a woman has painstakingly gone over the details and spent countless hours to ensure it.

The carefree dad and hyper-responsible mom is an odd-couple dynamic that is widely exploited in the media, especially in children's cartoons. Here, we often see storylines about how Dad can't do anything without Mom, and while these often seem to be poking fun at Dad, they also teach children to have very different expectations for their mothers and fathers. Dads aren't expected to anticipate anyone's needs, because that's Mom's job. Dad's parenting failures only make him more lovable—oh, he's such a goofball—and these episodes usually resolve with Dad expressing a newfound appreciation for Mom's worrying. But that's where it stops—with appreciation. There's no follow-up in the next episode, where Dad has resolved to worry about more so that Mom can worry about less.

Worry is an invisible load, and one that comes with little to no recognition. On the contrary, dads are often called in to be the problem solvers, which is visible work that comes with a high reward. There was a fire, Dad put it out, and now Dad's the hero! Dad! Dad! Dad! Dad! However, when Mom's worrying prevents the fire from happening in the first place, no one chants for Mom. If they notice Mom's work here at all, it's by being annoyed that she is so anti-candle.

Sadly, the only reward that mothers often get for all their years of worry—for being what they have been told is a "good" mom—is that, bluntly put, their children like them less. Dads are the relaxed parents, the parent who plays, who's fun to talk to and who is often actually present when they're present. Moms, on the other hand, are distracted and busy with how much they need to take care of. Worry is their love language, and that's all they know, but to their children, their worry often comes across as criticism and drives a wedge in the relationship. The curse of being a mom is worrying so much about the people you love that those people will someday no longer want to be around you because you're kind of a bummer.

It's a tragedy, really, and one that might worry us more if our worry bandwidth wasn't already so tapped out. I remember once reading a 2019 Facebook post from Elizabeth Gilbert where she recalled being at a conference where someone asked the question "How many of you are afraid of turning into your mother?" and nearly everyone in the room stood up. Going out on a limb (but don't worry, I'm being careful!), I think a lot of women feel like this because they can see that their mother has never had a relaxed day in her life, and that's not what they want for themselves. We don't want to find ourselves ultimately shunned for doing our duty, but at the same time, we don't know how to break the cycle. It is hard to know how to be relaxed, stress-free, and not worried if you have never had that modeled for you.

There are legitimate things to worry about, and to a certain degree, some amount of worry is part of being a responsible caretaker, but excessive, constant worry is different. This kind of worry is an affliction and addiction that we cannot control. We know that we should relax because that is what we need, but often we can't because we don't know how.

When you have lived with stress and worry your entire life, this is how you are most comfortable, and experiencing even just a moment of being worry-free feels unsafe. For most of my life, I felt like I was slacking or ungrateful if I wasn't worried about everything all the time. I still get a sick, anxious feeling when I buy something that isn't on sale or "a good deal," because I feel guilty that maybe I'm not as worried about money as I should be, and if I'm not worried about money, then surely I'm going to go broke any minute and then I'll really be miserable, so it's probably safer to just go ahead and make myself a little miserable now and not let myself enjoy the nice little thing that I can afford. Worry has always been part of how I "earned" the things that I loved and wanted, how I proved that I was worthy of them—from jobs and material goods to relationships—and so I worried that if I wasn't worried, then surely something was wrong and I didn't deserve the thing I wasn't worried about. I've also used worry as an amulet, believing that "the things you worry about never happen," and that if I put enough energy into worrying about how something might go bad, then I'll somehow be protected, or at least not so disappointed, when it does. As a habit and a practice, it is just as draining as it sounds.

Worrying is work that is never done, and it carries with it mental and physical exhaustion that is bringing us to a crisis point. Women are twice as likely to report depression and anxiety as men and a third more likely to experience burnout. We have to learn how to relax and break the cycle of worry, because our lives depend on it.

We might not have grown up with relaxation role models, but we can change that for our daughters and the generations of women who come after us. They deserve to know what a truly relaxed woman looks like, just like we deserve to *be* that woman. It's not easy to do this in a culture that expects and reinforces our willingness to worry for everyone, to take on more than our share. For women, relaxation has become an act of rebellion. To relax is to challenge everything we have been taught about how we should behave and to finally value ourselves and our well-being above others' expectations. We have to get comfortable with a certain amount of risk—the risk that people will think we are not pulling our weight, the risk that people will disapprove of or not like us, the risk that something bad might happen and that someone, somewhere might consider it our fault. That's scary, sure, but in my opinion, not nearly as scary as forty more years of self-punishment and denial of joy.

But how do we do it? How do we actually relax

instead of just trying to relax and then punishing ourselves when we fail? One of the first steps is to let ourselves off the hook for worrying by recognizing that a certain amount (but a certain amount only) is healthy. We often worry about things that are new and exciting because they're just that—new and exciting! We worry about the people we love because we love them. What we care about is what we worry about, and so it's not realistic to strive for a life with truly no worries. The problem is when our worries become scripts that run automatically, born from a sense of unworthiness or the belief that we haven't yet earned the right to enjoy the moment.

The first step to worrying less is paying attention and becoming aware of when we're responding to a real problem versus when we're just playing reruns (something bad is going to happen, you haven't earned this, you're responsible for everyone's feelings, etc.). Is there actually something to worry about, or are we worrying by default? Is the script we're running applicable or just familiar? Once you've identified a script, it's time for a rewrite that stokes calm instead of fear. It doesn't work to just tell yourself to not worry and then try to stamp out the worries as they show up. If we want those thoughts to go away, we have to be ready to fill the vacuum they leave behind or else it will fill itself, usually with more worries.

Many of us are used to an endless stream of negative thoughts chatting us up from morning till late at night. This is where statements of gratitude and affirmations can be very useful. Affirmations are often seen as cheesy, where we imagine someone looking in the mirror and saying, "I have a Louis Vuitton bag," because they believe that's somehow going to make one appear in their closet. But affirmations don't have to be so blunt and can actually be a subtle, powerful way to change worry scripts and break their incessant loops.

When your worries tell you everything is going to fall apart and it's all going to be your fault, your affirmations are right there, ready to go, reminding you that you are capable, that you've got this. When your worries start to tell you that you are bad, your affirmations can help remind you of your good. So many of us are wired to always be doing something, and using affirmations can be a way of working with instead of against yourself because they give your hungry brain something to chew on that just happens to be nutritious.

We can also use our worries as maps, leading us to the areas of our lives that we most care about. It's wondrous that we have friends, families, jobs, neighbors, pets, houses, cars. Everything, even the goddamn laundry, is really, if you think about it, something to be grateful for because it means that we have clothes! (Okay, so maybe I'm stretching it a bit here with the laundry, but you get my point.) Worry robs us of delight and presence, it takes us out of the now and thrusts us into a hyper loop where we're zooming from the past—where we're sure we didn't do enough to eradicate risk—to the future, a place where we will always feel powerless because it isn't real. Reframing the subjects of our worry into subjects of our gratitude can remind us that we are allowed to be in the moment and to appreciate what is happening right now.

I can't count the number of times I've hit the end of something, be it a party or a vacation or a yoga class or just a lovely summer afternoon, and have become overwhelmed with sadness at the realization that I spent the whole time thinking about something else. And by *thinking*, I mean *worrying*. The most heartbreaking instance of this, for me, is my first pregnancy, with my son. I spent nine months so miserable with worry about everything that could possibly go wrong and everything that I could do wrong that I thought I hated being pregnant. I can see now that I didn't hate being pregnant, I just hated being worried about being pregnant, and had I known that would be my only chance to carry a child that I would someday meet, I am sure I would have spent more time marveling at the wonder of his kicks and movements instead of anxiously counting them.

I don't want to miss out on my own life ever again,

and I finally love myself enough to believe that I can make presence my priority. It is okay for me to look up at the sky and down at the ground to remember where I am and what I'm doing, and just breathe. It is incredible how just pausing, and taking five deep breaths while thinking about breathing, does more to calm a worry than a flurry of text messages, an hour of sanitizing countertops, and eighty-seven dollars' worth of late-night panic buys ever could. A deep breath can also trigger gratitude, in that a lungful of air will often remind you just how grateful you are to be alive. The good thing about breathing is that you can always come back to it. Your lungs are always with you. The second you find yourself slipping, losing your grip on the now, don't worry about it—just breathe. Remind yourself that nothing is too good to be true, the other shoe does not always drop, your luck will not always run out. Sometimes good things happen and are meant to just be enjoyed. Yes, even by you.

Worry is not your job. It is not your penance. It is not how you pay for all the good in your life. It is just a habit, and habits can be broken. When a worry pops up, we can stop responding to it as if it is a call to action. We can stop trying to do things to assuage it or broadcast it to anyone who will listen. Instead, we can just recognize it for the intrusive thought that it is and send it on its way, no harm, no foul. This doesn't mean living in denial and telling yourself that the shit will never hit the fan. It means telling yourself that when it does, it will not automatically be your fault, and that you—you smart, capable, good person, you—will also know what to do. If needed, you will make a run for it, and the flight attendants will understand.

# 10

## Nothing Is Sacred

I got my first tattoo my senior year of college, when I was spending a semester studying Spanish in Mexico. Getting tattooed there was cheaper than getting tattooed in the United States, which was part of how I ended up with a dessert plate–size mermaid emblazoned on my back, cresting a wave slightly above, yet drifting into, tramp stamp territory.

Before I returned home, I sent my parents an email, telling them about the mermaid, figuring that it was easier to be honest and deal with the consequences than try to hide something that was going to be pretty much impossible to keep hidden. My dad adopted an air of "that was stupid" disappointment, referring to my new tattoo as my "smudge," while my mom was flat-out pissed. My sister, however, who had previously gotten in trouble for getting her own tramp stamp as soon as she turned eighteen, was beside herself with delight. Especially once I got home and she saw that not only was my mermaid huge but also topless. "Kate got a giant tattoo with boobs," she'd remind my parents anytime she felt like her decisions were coming under too much scrutiny.

I'd always been of the mindset that it was easier to ask forgiveness than permission, but in this case, it didn't really hold true, and my parents weren't all that forthcoming with the forgiveness. Because of this, I held off on getting my second tattoo for almost a year, until after I'd already gotten a job in New York and was planning to move. At the time, I was living with my best friend. Before I packed everything up, we got matching bats (an homage to Francesca Lia Block's *Weetzie Bat* books—'90s gurls 4eva) on the top of our left feet to commemorate our friendship and the fact that I was now moving 1,200 miles away.

Unlike the mermaid, this tattoo was small, and I figured I could easily keep it hidden (all I had to do was wear socks) in the week I was going to spend at my parents' house to finalize all the details of my move. But even though I did keep it hidden, my parents still found out. You see, I might have been a rebel, but I was still a type A, hyper-organized, high-functioning rebel. The kind of rebel who puts "get tattoo" on her to-do list, right under selling her old clothes and calling her new boss, and then accidentally leaves that to-do list out in the open for her mom to find.

And how did my mom, when she found that list, know that I had already gotten the tattoo?

Because I'd crossed it off, of course.

As a baby overachiever, I lived and died by to-do lists, which I started making in high school. At first, they were merely a vanity project, as looking at all my responsibilities, written out on a piece of paper, made me feel grown up (even if one of my tasks was "Rollerblade"). Crossing them off brought a sense of smug satisfaction—*Look at me being productive! Look how much I can accomplish in a day!* I felt important, like a person of consequence. My to-do lists were a small ballast against the outside world's incessant reminders that teenage girls were only slightly more significant than bugs. When, at forty-three, I was finally diagnosed with ADHD, my early fixation on productivity made even more sense, because those lists served as physical proof that I wasn't the lazy space cadet I was made out to be. So what if I slept until noon—look how much I accomplished once I did wake up!

As I got older, my management systems grew more complex and technological, but I continued to blast through my days. I prided myself on being a person who could "get shit done" and rarely worried about taking on too much, because I was sure I could handle it. Then I became a mother.

Breastfeeding, as I've recounted, was a disaster, but also a task that was never completed. There was nothing to check off, no feeling of satisfaction at seeing a job done, even if not well done, and there was always something to do—more pumping, more washing parts and bottles, more research to try to get to the bottom of why it wasn't working. We were also preparing to move at the time, and I had a looming book deadline, so when my son slept, I frantically wrote, or fielded calls from the real estate agent, house painter, stager, landscaper, and the guy from Taskrabbit I was trying to get to come clean out the garage. I kept crossing items off my list that I actually could cross off, never stopping to rest, because I didn't think I deserved it.

The worst part, though, was that I resented the baby—because tending to his needs kept me from really "accomplishing" anything. It's so heartbreaking to realize this now because I can see how skewed my perspective had become, that bonding with my baby felt like doing nothing. If I were ever granted one do-over in my life, this would be it: I would go back to those newborn days, sit on the couch with some dumb TV show on in the background, and do nothing but hold him.

Years later, I saw an Instagram post from writer

Stephanie Danler that hit me so hard it's still etched in my mind. She'd just had her first baby, and she shared a picture of a sign that her doula had taped up in the house. It said, simply, "This is productive." My first reaction to seeing this was sheer jealousy, in that I wished I'd had someone in my life, at that point, to provide such a loving reminder of the value of caregiving. My second thought was more complicated and along the lines of *Oh god, what's happened to us?* Clearly, I wasn't alone in struggling to feel productive as a new mom. Going by the Oxford definition of *productive*, which is "producing or able to produce large amounts of goods, crops, or other commodities," it is hard to imagine anything more productive than bringing new life into the world and then nurturing it so that it can grow. And yet, from deep within a capitalist structure that assigns worth based on measurable output, we are made to feel like this alone is not enough.

The problem with productivity is that it prizes quantity over quality. It's a hamster wheel, which holds the promise of everything you want and need—accomplishment, self-worth, relaxation—at some point in a future that may never actually come. Such a focus on productivity also inevitably invites failure, because no matter how much you get done, there will always be more to do. Your inbox is a perfect example that has both a literal and metaphorical application.

Clearing your inbox means sending emails, but sending emails just results in more emails, which means your inbox will never get to zero for long enough for it to mean anything. The slate is never totally cleared, the to-do list is never totally crossed off, to the point where managing it becomes its own to-do. An entire industry of productivity-enhancing goods has arisen as a way to help us deal with this problem, and while some of them may help us get through the day, they also mask the fact that most of us don't really need to be more productive. Most of us need to do less, not find something to help us do more.

And yet too much has become the norm to the point where just enough now feels akin to nothing. This feeling is particularly acute for women, who are used to doing too much because they have too much to do. More than three-quarters of women in the United States between the ages of twenty-five and forty-four work outside of the home, yet women still do two and a half times the amount of unpaid labor as men. I do know a few families where the husband has adopted the role of primary caregiver while his wife works, but far and away, the majority of women I know work full-time and also manage almost all, if not all, of the household and childcare responsibilities. I also know many who are in charge of tasks like financial planning and bill paying and house repairs—tasks that, just a generation ago, were largely managed by men. Our culture, by and large, still thinks that there is such a thing as "women's work" and that it should therefore be left for us to do. And what is "women's work"? Well, pretty much anything and everything that has not been explicitly assigned to someone else.

I'm reminded here of Shel Silverstein's poem about Sarah Cynthia Sylvia Stout, who would not take the garbage out. Silverstein tells us that Sarah Cynthia Sylvia Stout already washes the dishes and scrubs the pans, cooks the yams and spices the hams, and yet when she refuses to do anything about the garbage, it piles up to the ceiling and finally the sky. Eventually, there's so much garbage that she gets buried in it and dies. "But children, remember Sarah Stout, and always take the garbage out" is the moral conclusion of the poem. We are told that her death by cellophane from old bologna and rubbery, blubbery macaroni is her own fault because she didn't do the thing that she was expected to do. As for all those people who watched her suffocate and did nothing to help, well, there is no moral for them! What were they supposed to do—take the garbage out themselves? No! Ew! Everyone knew that was Sarah Cynthia Sylvia Stout's job!

Many women I know have found that even when responsibilities are explicitly assigned in the household, it still falls on them to make sure things get done, and the mental load of project management is perhaps the weightiest load of all. Women have been taught that we should try extra hard to not be a burden, so we feel bad about outright asking someone else to do something. We often feel like, if we have to ask, then we have already failed. And yet, we try. I've seen task lists and chore charts (some beautifully illustrated by artist friends) and heard of project management software deployed to keep track of who is supposed to do what and by when, or decks of cards to gamify it, but I know no one who has found that any of these methods has resulted in what she wants, which is the automation in which someone else identifies what needs to be done and then just, you know, does it. "It'd be great if you did a few more things around the house," she says. "Sure! Make me a list," he says amicably and with earnestness, then wonders why she has jumped out the window.

For many of us, this unequal distribution of unpaid labor has come as kind of a shock. We were raised to believe in equality, and so we thought that things were going to be . . . um . . . more equal. Crazy, right? So many of us continue to try to delegate and share the load because we are tired of folding the laundry but also because we think that's what we should do.

I have a lot of conversations with women I know about unequal household duties, but if it sounds like we're having no-holds-barred bitch sessions about our male partners, we are not. Instead, these stories come out in bits and pieces, and more often than not, there is a little bit of shame attached to them. We're not ashamed of our partners, though. Instead, we're ashamed of ourselves and feel like we have failed because we have decided it is easier to just throw in the towel (to the washing machine) and do the laundry ourselves.

As with so many things, the unequal distribution of housework and childcare isn't just about the unequal distribution of housework and childcare. It's about the fact that while millennial and Gen X women were being raised to believe that we could have it all, society on the whole was not making dramatic changes and shifting responsibilities around to make this happen. If a woman wanted to have a career, more power to her! No one was going to lie down in front of her car to keep her from driving to work in the morning, but that alone is far from sufficient. Truly supporting someone requires a lot more than just not getting in her way, and for women to actually have it all, men must sacrifice more so that we can sacrifice less. We have to be brutally honest with ourselves here, though, that the division of unpaid labor is primarily a one-sided conversation that men, for the most part, aren't interested in joining. Women read and write books about the subject. They talk about it with their friends. They listen to podcasts. They invest time and thought and effort into how they might make things more equitable, and men ... aren't doing any of that.

Even with dramatic cultural shifts, housework will never be the lightning rod issue for men that it is for women because men have never been taught that their ability to keep house is reflective of their value as a person. Many of us who grew up in the '80s and '90s witnessed the women in our lives live in fear that someone might drop by unannounced. I have several friends who recall being dispatched to stand on the front porch and concoct reasons why unexpected visitors weren't allowed in the front door. The message we got was that anything less than a company-ready home was shameful. It's hard not to let that mentality influence your choices, especially if you are prone to overachievement. The best we can do, I think, is to remind ourselves that our home should be our sanctuary. Its purpose is to provide comfort and safety—not another platform by which you must demonstrate how worthy you are of being alive.

You are allowed to keep it to your standards or to not keep it at all. I'll never forget the first time I visited a neighbor and she met me at the door with a gin and tonic and said, "Just so you know, I don't clean." It was a refreshing change from the usual string of apologies.

Like so many areas of our life, our home is a place where we must get comfortable with a little bit (and occasionally, a lot) of mess and sometimes let things be as they are instead of tirelessly working to make them how we think they should be. Clean countertops aren't always worth staying up late. In a pinch, bikini bottoms are a perfectly fine substitute for underwear, and friends are coming by to see you, not the inside of your hamper. It's not women's work—it's just work— and sometimes, it's okay for the work not to get done.

Frankly, it often feels like we barely get to spend enough time enjoying the benefits of the home we so tirelessly work to keep because we are in fact never there. We're too busy! Far and away, the busiest people I know are parents (usually moms) who manage their kids' packed calendars. Between keeping track of and shuttling to and from soccer practices, gymnastics, choir, birthday parties, science fairs, and everything else on the calendar, these parents seem to have little time for their own lives or interests. While it used to be unheard of for a seven-year-old to have a packed calendar, it seems to be the norm for a lot of kids I know. Sometimes, people are aware of just how intense this is. ("I wake up every morning and think, *How am I going to do all of this?*" one friend said to me. "And I don't even have a job!") Others just accept it as the price to pay for a full life. They're exhausted, and no one really appears happy about how much there is to do, but everyone they know is doing it, so they can't imagine it any other way.

Keeping kids busy with activities can be a necessary form of childcare for working parents, but it can also be representative of how, like so many other things in our lives, we're doing so much not because we really want to but because we're scared of what will happen if we don't. We worry that the one opportunity we don't give to our children will be the one they feel like they missed out on. My friend who told me she wakes up every morning wondering how she's going to do it all also shared that her own childhood is her motivation. "I loved playing soccer, and I had the chance to be on a competitive team that traveled on the weekends," she said. "But my mom was like, 'What? No, we go to the lake on the weekends.'"

A few days later, another friend was telling me why she drew the line at one hour of after-school gymnastics a week for her son. "I played competitive soccer as a kid," she explained. "And every weekend, we were traveling and staying in shitty motels. I never got the chance to just hang out."

It's a hard truth that our children will probably resent us no matter what we do, or don't do, for them. That is their job. It is their job to look at what we did and think that they can do better. That's depressing in a lot of ways, but it also might make you feel a little better about saving a slice of yourself for yourself and finding a point where your kids are busy and happy and you're not a spent shell with a numb butt because you've been driving back and forth across town for the last four hours.

This point, I guess, could be that thing called *balance*, that thing we're told is the holy grail that will solve all our problems but which we know does not actually exist. Our modern lives aren't so much a balance beam as they are some crazy *American Ninja Warrior* course where the tiniest thing can send us tumbling down. The concept of balance also somehow turns systemic failures into personal failures (a woman's personal failures, to be precise) and makes us believe that it's not that we have so much to do but that we're just bad at doing it all.

The closest you'll get to balance is to just not try to do everything. Get comfortable with the feeling that you're missing out, that your kids are missing out. When that FOMO comes up, instead of letting it propel you to leave soccer fifteen minutes early so you can get to choir fifteen minutes late, just recognize it and let it go. You can't do it all, no matter how hard you try, so sit back, if you can, and enjoy what you are doing.

As a culture, we are quite judgmental about free

and unstructured time and often work to fill any open slots on our calendar. Not too long ago, I turned down a playdate at the zoo—a thirty-minute drive west—on a Saturday morning because, that same day, we already had plans to go to a skating party that was a forty-five-minute drive east. "Oh yes, we're going to that, too," the other mother, who lives only a few blocks away, told me. "But that's not until the afternoon."

Over the past few years, I've made a concerted effort to unbusy myself. I'm careful about what I say yes to and pay close attention to making sure our weekends are largely unscheduled. Some of my favorite things we have done as a family have been spontaneous ones that came up last minute, like a rainy-day visit to a car museum or an afternoon where all three of us sat at the table and painted. But I have to admit that, at the same time, it has left us socially out of step. We're always open to barbecues and park hangs, but since nobody else is, those rarely happen. On the off chance that they do, I sometimes find myself feeling like I can't join the conversation, because it's so often centered around just how busy everyone is.

I've also been processing a certain amount of grief about the fact that the childhood I wanted for my son just might not be possible anymore. When I think about growing up, what I think about the most is all those times when I had nothing to do. How my friends and I would walk to one particular gas station every day after school because that was the one where the gummy bears were so old they had hardened, and we liked them that way. The smell of a hardware store will be forever nostalgic because I went there so often with my dad, strolling the aisles to pick out screws, because what else did I have to do? I remember the shimmer of hot parking lots, the sound of silence in the summer, and the pleasant disorientation that comes from waking up after falling asleep on the trampoline. It was this sense of time being infinitely squanderable because there was just so much of it. It taught me that nothing is sacred, and yet I don't know that people do nothing anymore.

We didn't just wake up one day and choose to be this busy. Rather, we've arrived here after decades of being herded in this direction by capitalism, a herding that increased dramatically in intensity with the arrival of social media because now even our leisure time can be quantified by likes. I can't help but think, though, that all of this rushing to make sure we don't miss out is actually causing us to miss out on everything. Our days, weeks, months, and years go by in a blur. We rush through whatever we are doing so that we can hurry and get to the next thing, only to rush through that as well.

If you've ever had a day where you honestly can't really remember what you did, it might be because no matter what you were doing, you were always thinking about what you were going to do next. I've often found myself rushing through brushing my teeth so I can rush through getting dressed so I can rush through breakfast to rush through the drive to school so that I can rush through work and then rush through errands and . . . I'm literally rushing through every single aspect of my day. In the back of my head, I'm thinking that I'm doing this so I can sit down and read a book at some point, but that opportunity doesn't come until the end of the day, usually after nine o'clock at night if it comes at all. So am I literally just trying to get through fourteen hours of my day with the hopes I'll be able to be present for the final sixty minutes? That's just sad.

If you don't take the time to define your priorities for yourself, then someone—or something—else will define them for you. I have to constantly remind myself that my ultimate, number one goal in my life right now is to pay attention to what I am doing rather than just automatically trying to do more. I've noticed that I always get a dip in my mood right when I get home from picking my son up from school. I walk in the house, and there is so much to get done. I probably chose to forgo running errands but still didn't do as much work as I would have liked. Even if I cleaned up after myself after lunch, the sink is full of dishes because the dishwasher needs to be emptied. The trash is overflowing and the recycling needs to be taken out. Putting away school clothes reminds me of the pile of laundry and the fact that the towels need to be washed—again. The dogs destroyed a toy and so there is fuzz everywhere. My mom called that morning and I need to call her back to plan a weekend visit, and I have several unreturned texts about school stuff, work stuff, and appointments, and a coworker I haven't seen in a decade sent me a meme and I want to let him know that I'm honored that he still associates midforties me with teenage witches. I need to bring in and sort the mail, and dinner is only a few hours away. What are we going to eat? I am overwhelmed by where to start, and so I don't start at all.

Instead, I make a snack. We go sit on the porch or by the fire. I tell my son I saw a fox that day, and we yell at a squirrel to get away from the bird feeder. He finds a stick and a rubber band, and I do my best to turn them into a bow and arrow. Everything else can wait, because time passes really quickly even when you're trying to take it slow.

# 11

## Agree to Think You're Really Pretty

I went most of middle school without looking in the mirror. I could have been walking around with an entire toaster strudel stuck in my teeth, but that was better than the alternative: getting caught glancing at my reflection and having those who caught me decide that I was looking because I liked what I saw. I couldn't imagine anything worse than having other people think that I thought that I was pretty. In junior high, having a reputation for thinking that you were pretty was akin to social death. At my school, it was also a recipe for literally getting your ass kicked.

More so than it was a place to actually relieve oneself, the girls' bathroom was the spot to skip class and hang out. If you walked in to find it empty, you could breathe a sigh of relief. Otherwise, you did your business as quickly and quietly as possible, washed your hands, and got out, all while staring at the sink or the floor. Anywhere, really, so long as it was not the mirror, or the group of girls evading gym class by hanging out in the corner. Let everyone know that you believed yourself a troll, and you were probably gonna be okay.

I wish I could say that this type of behavior was rewarded only in the festering jungle that is middle school, but it's not. In our culture, across generations, we still take an unkind view toward a woman who thinks she looks good or thinks that there is anything good about herself at all. Self-hatred, and listing ways in which you, your body, and your life are deficient, is a compulsory part of female bonding. In *Sex and the City*, the fab four eat takeout and discuss how unbeautiful they are. Charlotte says, "Ooooo, I hate my thighs!" Miranda doesn't like her chin, and Carrie her nose. When the three turn expectantly to Samantha to list her flaws, they're met with silence. Finally, Samantha says, "I happen to like the way I look," to which Miranda retorts, "You should—you paid enough for it!" Then everyone has a good laugh at Samantha's expense, because why spare her feelings when she doesn't have the decency to put herself down?

We're taught early on that the only correct way to respond to a compliment is to defer, and we've all been Cady Heron, trying to instantaneously decipher a com-

pliment so that we can respond appropriately: How ve-
hemently must we deny, and how hard are we going
to be punished if we don't? It's no coincidence (but it
is a good joke) that in that other iconic pink movie,
when "all problems of feminism have been solved," the
Barbies don't just give out compliments with glee, but
receive them as well.

Growing up in the Midwest in the '80s and '90s, I
was taught that low self-esteem was a form of polite-
ness so important that it almost veered into morality,
at least for women. There were a lot of good cooks in
my family, and yet a meal was rarely served without
an accompanying list of ways in which it could have
been better and did not turn out quite as well as the
cook had hoped. When visiting someone's house for
the first time, the wife/mom would almost certainly
apologize for it being a disaster—even if the carpet
still bore the pattern of vacuum marks and the mantel
boasted not a speck of dust—and then list off things
that were breaking, that needed to be replaced, or that
she absolutely hated.

This form of polite self-loathing and flaw-focusing
was most extreme, though, when it came to oneself, and
especially the size of one's body. Most adult women I
knew were always on some sort of diet, and calorie
restriction was always a popular topic of conversation.
I remember once standing in a shop with my mom

as she chatted with the shopkeeper, a woman she had been acquainted with for some years. "You know," the woman said, "all I ate yesterday was half a sandwich, and I didn't lose a single pound!" That conversation has stuck with me because even though I was still in elementary school at the time, I already knew that that wasn't how weight loss worked. Looking back as an adult, I can see that it wasn't really about losing weight as much as it was about a semi-public show of self-denial. A willingness to starve, at least for a day, to make sure everyone knew how little you thought you were worth.

By second grade, I was already talking to my classmates about how I hated my thighs. I had decided that the fact that they spread out a bit when I sat down meant that they must be too big, but more than that, it was a bid to be liked. I wanted to fit in, and be popular, and so announcing to anyone who would listen that I was trying to lose weight seemed like a good way to do so. When sitting in class, I'd bounce my legs up and down under my desk so that everyone would know how serious I was, until one day, a kid named Tony walked by and saw my jittering knees. "Geez," he said, totally annoyed with me. "You're not that fat!" Point taken. I gave it up, realizing that nonstop exercising didn't quite make me as likable as I had hoped.

The idea that low self-esteem is a good thing is continually reinforced in pop culture, and the girl/woman who doesn't know she is beautiful has been elevated to goddess status. One Direction sings, "You don't know you're beautiful, oh, oh-oh / That's what makes you beautiful." And because I have '90s country songs burned into my brain for all eternity ("Mary Ann and Wanda were the best of friends, all through their high school days . . ."), I still remember Sammy Kershaw singing, "She don't know she's beautiful (no, she's not that kind)." For these women, real or fictional, we are meant to interpret her unawareness of her own beauty as proof of her purity and her humility. She's the good kind of girl, not the bad kind. You know, the kind that thinks she's hot shit.

For celebrity women, who often owe much of their career to their beauty, it has become a required talking point to discuss their insecurities and/or how ugly and awkward they used to be when they were young. Maybe it's the influencer who says she only got fillers because she was so insecure about her thin lips, the iconic supermodel who thinks she's bow-legged, the pop star with a "flat" butt, thin brows, broad shoulders, lanky legs, big ears, a too-hairy hairline. The idea is that sharing these insecurities shows that *Celebs! They're just like us!* Part of this, surely, is that we expect successful women to pay some sort of penance by denying their gifts, but it also sends the message that being dissatisfied with yourself is normal, all simply part of being a woman.

I believe that a lot of this starts out as false modesty. We actually think we are pretty, or that we are good at something, or that we are smart, but we deny this to others because we know that this is the polite thing to do. We deny it so much, though, that we start to believe it, and soon, we really do think that we look awful and that we can't do anything well or right. For us to believe that there is anything good about us, we need to hear it from someone else, and so we get locked in a pattern of basing our self-worth on external validation.

Unfortunately, such validation can be hard to come by, something that we're always seeking yet rarely finding. As kids, many of us had at least one adult in our lives who worried that we might get a "big head" if we were offered too much praise. Many people seemed to believe that confidence was somehow toxic to a child's development and would often go out of their way to make sure young people had a clear view of their shortcomings. Maybe you weren't ever told you looked nice but were told when you didn't. Maybe if you were proud of your 90 percent on a test, someone would say, "Well, you still got two wrong," or they frequently pointed out the even greater accomplishments of other kids your age.

I think our caregivers intended for this treatment to serve as a protective measure, as they assumed that a kid who thought they were worthy of something extra would grow up with a sense of entitlement that would leave them forever disappointed. Reminding us of our shortcomings was meant to instill us with a sense of hard work, but the end result was that many of us ended up feeling like no matter how good we did, or were, we could always try to do, or be, better. Instead of ending up with a dreaded "big head," many of us were left with a sense of smallness that we're still trying to overcome even well into adulthood.

This isn't to blame anyone else in particular, just to illustrate one of the many ways in which our society preaches confidence while secretly believing that—at least for girls—confidence will only lead to problems. It doesn't, though. I remember having a friend whose parents thought she hung the moon. As a result, she thought that of herself, even though she was actually pretty average across the board. She wasn't the most popular girl in high school, as some people were kind of turned off by her extreme confidence, but this didn't seem to bother her. In fact, I'm not sure she even noticed. We recently reconnected after losing touch for many years, and I was shocked at how her life turned out. Because, you guys, she was fine! Better than fine, even! She has a graduate degree and works in a field that she loves, she has been married to the same man for almost twenty years, and, he clearly thinks she hung the moon, too. She thinks her kids are the best thing to ever happen to planet Earth, and they think the same of their mom. I've seen her parents lately, too, and they still think she's the greatest! She's probably one of the happiest people I know.

I'm sure some people are reading this now and thinking, *Well, no one should think that highly of themselves, and it's only going to come back and bite those kids in the*... But just stop. Why are we, as a culture, so scared of people, especially women, having confidence? Not I'm-a-bad-bitch do-it-for-the-'gram faux confidence, but genuine self-worth? What is so bad about it? I still know parents now who deliberately don't compliment their kids, and it is very easy to find parenting advice that backs this up. It's like we're worried our kids might think they're special and then someday enter the "real world," where they will be devastated to find out they are not. When it comes to learning that they ain't all that, we'd rather our kids hear it from us, and sooner rather than later.

But how does setting people up for a lifetime of low self-esteem protect them from anything? It doesn't, but it does protect the flawed systems that need people to believe that they must work themselves to the bone to earn the right to try to buy themselves back. This is especially acute for women, who are constantly being told that what will save us from all of this overextension and overachievement and overwork and burnout is—wait for it, wait for it—self-care. I'll pause here for a second so that we can all have a moment of rolling on the floor in a rueful fit of laughter, because at this point in time, the concept of self-care as we are being sold it is kind of a joke. It's not funny, but it's still a joke, because what does self-care even mean anymore?

To be a woman in the world (basically, a woman who consumes anything at all) at this point in time is to find yourself smack-dab in the middle of an inspirational clusterfuck. It's as if, at some point in time in the last couple of decades, the powers that be got together and decided that it was lack of imagination that was holding women back. Clearly, we just didn't believe in ourselves enough, and so we needed every advertisement, every article, every post, every influencer, every bit of packaging to remind us that we should be going for our dreams and living our best lives.

Paper towels are no longer marketed as just being good for cleaning up spills. Instead, they come loud and clear with the message that these paper towels will help you have it all because once you clean up that spill, you can get back to being that badass that you know you are! Bras are no longer just about supporting our breasts but supporting us on our grind! That influencer isn't just posting about those bedsheets because she's getting paid to but because she wants you to know that if you sleep on these sheets, then you, too, can wake up ready to take on your insanely busy day! #sponsored #ad

And when it comes to how we look and our appearances, well, forget it. Every beauty service and product is now referred to as *self-care*, which has rebranded the process of trying to meet impossible beauty standards as something that we do not because we feel pressured but because it makes us feel good! Waxing? Self-care. Punishing exercise classes? Self-care. Cosmetic procedures that still have you writhing on the table even after a liberal application of numbing cream? Self-care, baby! A friend recently messaged me about a sign she'd seen in her Brooklyn neighborhood: "Celebrate Women's History Month with 30% Off Lip Fillers!" You can't make this up.

What we're left with is an increasingly long list of "self-care" chores that we feel compelled to do and a mounting sense of dissatisfaction—and guilt—that doing them doesn't actually make us feel cared for. A while back, I was sitting near the galley on a long flight, and I eavesdropped on the conversation between two flight attendants of difference races and generations, as they discussed the pressure to keep up with their appearance. The older woman compared the hours she spent getting highlights and laser hair removal to the twenty minutes, every six weeks, that it took her husband to get a haircut. The younger woman said that she'd stopped getting her nails done because it had become "the monkey on my back" whenever she had any free time. It was what she felt like she should do, even though going to sit at the salon was the last thing she actually wanted to do. I could identify with both of them, as I've had more weekends than I can count where I squeezed in a manicure—in a crowded, hectic, loud environment—on a Saturday morning only to feel like I had no right to be exhausted come Sunday night, or annoyed with my husband for taking a whole day to go fishing, because I'd had my me time, too.

We have also bought whole-hog into the idea that self-care is not so much a necessity as it is a "treat" or a "reward." A reward is something that you earn and a treat is something that is out of the ordinary, so this is how we've been conditioned to see self-care and self-kindness—something we earn and that doesn't happen all that often. We have to wrench the idea of self-care away from luxury marketers and instead start treating it as what it really is: something that cannot be bought. True self-care is making sure your basic needs (sleep, food, movement) are met on a daily basis. Self-care is setting boundaries, even when they make people uncomfortable, so that you are not doing more than you can sustain. It is not something that you do for an hour on a Saturday morning but something that you do constantly, from the time you open your eyes in the morning until you close them at night. Self-care is valuing yourself as you are now and allowing yourself to feel good even—gasp!—if you're not perfect.

When we are constantly being exposed to stuff that is supposed to make us feel better, we are meant to assume that we feel bad. This is not wrong, but what is wrong is that we have been conditioned to believe that feeling bad about ourselves and our lives is normal. We have come to believe that it is a given that women exist in various states of self-loathing. Content geared toward men is often something along the lines of "15 Hacks to Be Even More Awesome Than You Already Are!" Women get "187 Ways to Try to Stop Feeling Like Garbage." That stuff sinks in, and we start to think that if everyone else feels bad about themselves, then who are we to feel good?

For much of human history, fitting in and being accepted was a matter of survival because it meant that you got to live in the camp with other people instead of in the wilderness, alone with the bears. It's still like that today, in that research has shown that the people who are most likely to survive a disaster are not the ones who have the most beans stockpiled in their basements but those who have the strongest networks of friends and neighbors. On a base level, it is safer to be a part of the group, and so if the group feels bad, then it's no surprise why feeling good seems so risky.

There's also a sinister subliminal message to the idea of self-care, especially for women, because it serves as a subtle reminder that we must care for ourselves because we cannot expect anyone else to do so. Sadly, this is true for a lot of us, in that if we don't care for ourselves, then no one will care for us at all. Much like the idea of balance, the idea of self-care removes all responsibility from society and places it on the individual woman. When we fall apart, it's our fault, because we probably weren't taking care of ourselves. One of the many vicious catch-22s that women must navigate is that it's hard to truly take care of yourself when you don't feel like you deserve it. But then, the less you take care of yourself, the less you feel like you deserve to do so. Argh! We can't win.

It is a great and evil irony that we live in a world that is constantly telling us that the more we hate ourselves, the more lovable we become to other people. It's no small feat to resist this, but it is possible. We don't have to think we're the best. We just have to stop thinking we're the worst. We have to give ourselves props to prop ourselves up, dish out compliments and take them. We can get manicures because we want red nails, not because we think those nails are going to make up for the fact that we haven't had enough sleep or are overwhelmed with to-dos. We can stop trying so hard to eradicate stray hairs or fine lines or cellulite or dark circles or any of the other ten million things that we're always being told we must fix before we love ourselves because we no longer believe that our bodies are just a mess of problems to be solved.

None of us are going to feel good about ourselves 100 percent of the time, but if we can bring awareness to how often we reflexively view ourselves with disdain, we can try to consciously scale back on doing so. We can decide that we have a right to look in the mirror and like what we see, even if someone else might catch us doing so. We can support other women who do the same, and even though our feet are flat, when someone tells us we look pretty, we can say, "Thanks, I know! And so do you!" And we can mean it.

# 12

## Acceptance Isn't Settling

We already have a dog," I responded to my sister when she texted me a pic of a flyer from her vet's office.

"C'mon," she wrote back. "How are you going to say no to this chocolate chunk?" I clicked open the photo again and enlarged it. He was indeed chocolatey. He was indeed chunky, all belly rolls and leg wrinkles at nine weeks old.

"What's the number?" I wrote to my sister. She sent it to me. "We might just go look," I wrote back.

"Sure you will," she said. We both knew that what I'd written was a lie.

The whole time I had been trying to get pregnant, I had winnowed my life, studiously avoiding anything that I thought might add work or complication. Even when it came to good things, my default was to avoid them if they weren't absolutely necessary. I didn't start any new work projects, didn't travel, said no to most social obligations, all in a bid to keep things as stress-free as possible. During that time, something as extravagant as a puppy would have been out of the question. I would have dismissed it immediately as "too much work."

But in the months after we stopped trying, I began to see the results of my single focus. I had worried so much about stress that I stressed about everything. I had stopped having fun. I'd kept things so simple that they'd gotten boring, held so much space that I created a vacuum that could not be filled by yin yoga alone. And there was no denying that even though the chocolate chunk had four legs and a tail, he was still what I had spent the last three years wanting more than anything in the world: another baby.

Three days and $800 later, we were driving home with him in my lap, licking my face and farting so much it made my eyes water. We named him Harry, and from minute one, Harry seemed to know and understand that he was Harry. He couldn't get up the back stairs on his own, but once lifted up, he walked in the house like he owned the place and immediately peed on the floor. Our dog Clem, easily three times Harry's size, cowered under the dining room table, but Harry was undeterred. In fact, undeterred was pretty much Harry's approach to everything. He ate like he'd never been fed and figured out how to get on the couch all on his own—with a full-speed run and then launching himself off the ottoman, ears and feet and tongue flying in every direction.

It had been more than thirty years since I'd had a puppy, and what I remembered from my childhood was that you put them in a cardboard box with a ticking clock to keep them calm. Harry gave a fuck about a cardboard box or a ticking clock, however, howling puppy howls at the top of his lungs, then pooping and stepping in it, which necessitated an immediate bath that got him clean and me dirty, and a removal of the cardboard box to the garbage. That night, my husband slept on the couch next to Harry and the next morning looked and felt like he hadn't slept at all. Harry, on the other hand, was as fresh as a daisy, at least until he peed again and tracked it all over the kitchen.

Much of my dreaming about another baby was centered around my son having a sibling, his joy and excitement when we brought a new little brother or sister home from the hospital, the pride he'd experience and the attention he'd get when he got to share the news at school, the love and bonding. When we stopped trying, these were the things that were the hardest to let go of, the most difficult admission to process that no matter how much I wanted to give my child everything, I couldn't. I knew that this might be the closest he ever got to experiencing what it was like to welcome a new family member, and my heart swelled at seeing how happy he was with the new addition.

"Harry is so cute," he would say, and after a few days, he declared that Harry was his dog, though he wanted to make sure we knew that this did not mean that he was going to feed or help clean up after him. Harry grew like bamboo and, within a couple of months, weighed more than our other dog and our son, and it was extremely gratifying to see how the relationship they were developing was truly sibling-like. Our only child now had competition for food and for toys, and came to quickly understand what it was like to have your sandwich nommed and your stuffie stolen in the three seconds you turned your back.

Our son delighted in being the disciplinarian—"Harry! In your crate now!"—and yet was also fiercely protective when anyone else tried to do the same. "Do not yell at Harry! That is my dog!" Or crying when I loudly declared no more treats after Harry nipped my fingers, taking one not-so-nice. "You can't do that! Harry needs food to survive!"

His preschool teacher had once unknowingly broken my heart when she shared that he had asked if he was the only one in the class who didn't have a brother or a sister, because he worried he shouldn't be at that school if he was. But now we talked about how we were a family of five that just happened to have fourteen feet, and bringing Harry to preschool pickup engendered more attention and excitement than any human baby. One night, we sat on the bed as my son counted his toes. "Daddy toe, mommy toe, brother toe, sister toe, baby toe," he said, moving down the line. "Yes," I said. "Or daddy toe, mommy toe, you toe, Clem toe, Harry toe." He beamed.

Harry might not have been the baby I wanted, but he's the baby I got, and his arrival completed our little family. There is still more that I want and ways that I wish things were different, but on the whole, I'm pretty satisfied with my life these days. I feel blessed and grateful, though by conventional standards, I should not feel this way. When you exist inside a culture that tells you to never stop trying and to pursue your dreams at all costs, then making do with anything other than what you had aspired to is merely settling. Settling is nothing to be grateful for and certainly nothing to be celebrated. But I'm not settling, I'm accepting, even of the fact that Harry ate my UGGs.

*Acceptance* and *settling* are two different things. Acceptance is admitting to yourself that perfection does not exist. Settling is believing that perfection does exist, just not for you. A fear of settling can motivate you to keep trying in pursuit of that perfection. Acceptance is letting go. Settling is giving up. Acceptance is expansive and lets you look in wonder at a whole wide world of possibilities. Settling is narrowing and keeps you focused on what you do not have. Acceptance is something that you choose to practice, while settling is something that you do when you don't feel like you have any other choice.

The biggest difference between the two, though, is not in how it looks from the outside but how it feels on the inside. Acceptance feels freeing, like lightening your load. Often, when you accept something, it becomes easier to move forward. Settling, on the other hand, feels like carrying a burden, and rather than moving on, it can keep you stuck in the same place as you continue to resent what you have and focus on what you don't. There's no definitive checklist you can follow to know when you're accepting and when you're settling, which leaves both concepts ripe for twisting and exploitation.

Throughout our lives, we've heard a lot about settling. We shouldn't settle for less than the best, less than we deserve, anything but everything we've ever wanted. We're led to believe that the righteous path is one of rejection, believing that the only way to get what we want out of life is to remain closed off to everything that is not exactly what we want lest we accidentally settle. On the contrary, we're taught that acceptance is . . . well, actually who knows, because we aren't taught much about acceptance at all. This is because our entire society is built upon capitalism, which needs you to reject what you have while pursuing what you do not. There is a lot of profit to be made when we decide that who we are and what we have are not sufficient, and hardly any off us looking around and deciding, *Nah, it's cool, I'm good.* Capitalism wants you to accept nothing and resist everything, because then you will try to be someone else and have something different. And, more often than not, when you're trying, you're buying. The idea is that if you're not constantly trying to acquire more, then you are settling for less, and if you're settling for less, then it goes without saying that you, too, must not measure up.

When we're so used to rejecting everything that comes our way, we do the same thing with ourselves. Once again, we're taught this at an early age. We learn that only parts of us are acceptable, and even then, those parts need constant work and monitoring to remain so. We try to vanquish the less-than-perfect parts of ourselves and often dangle self-love as the carrot at the end of the stick. We just need to keep going, work a little harder, be strict and disciplined with ourselves, and then when we're finally perfect, we think, we can start to accept who we are.

Because we think we can only accept ourselves when we're perfect, we think that acceptance is basically making a statement of our own perfection and who are we to be so bold? But acceptance isn't about denying the fact that something could be better. Rather, it's seeing that something could be better without believing that it has to be and seeing improvement as a choice that can be made as opposed to a path that must be followed. We are not obligated to constantly be working on ourselves. If we want, we can just let things be, even our imperfections, and this doesn't mean that we're not doing the work. Sometimes, especially for overachievers, this is the work.

We might think that acceptance means welcoming something with open arms. Really, though, acceptance simply means acknowledging something for what it is, flaws and all, while letting go of how you thought it should be. Acceptance doesn't mean that you have to delude yourself into thinking that what you got was somehow what you really wanted all along or that you never wanted anything in the first place. You are allowed to want things that you do not get. You are allowed to continue to want them long after you have accepted that you might never get them. Acceptance is not a magic act that transforms the disappointment and pain from your past into something that no longer hurts, nor does it protect you from ever experiencing pain again. You can even accept something and still wish it were not so. Accepting is simply recognizing that it is what it is and no longer spending time and energy trying to make it into something it is not.

A lot of the time, resistance seems to come so much easier than acceptance because it's all we know. It feels safer to fight than to surrender, no matter what we're up against, because we've been in so many situations where fighting was a matter of survival. For most of human history, women have been offered scraps and been expected to accept them gratefully. The fact that we didn't, that we're still refusing the pittances that we're offered, is probably the reason we have anything at all. The problem is that, like trying, resistance is a good thing that becomes bad when we cling to it out of habit and automatically resist everything that we think we might not want rather than allowing ourselves to be open to something that we might not have expected.

Fear can be another motivator for rejection and resistance. We are scared of something, and so we don't want to let it into our lives. The only thing we can do with fear is accept that, to a certain degree, we're stuck with it. When we accept that we cannot forever vanquish fear, we can move from living in fear to living with it. When we live in fear, we let our fears dictate what we do. We turn fear into our dungeon master, a tyrant that dictates our every move and keeps us forever in the basement, away from the light. When we live in fear, we buy the ticket but don't take the ride. When we live with fear, we climb aboard. We buckle up and remind ourselves that it's okay to scream.

Self-acceptance is at the foundation of all acceptance, but when many of us hear about self-acceptance, we laugh. *Yeah, sounds great. Of course I'd love to do that. But how?* It seems so impossible, and it is when it is approached as a big blanket, a one-fell-swoop kind of thing. But when you start small, it's not quite so hard. Pick one thing about yourself that has always bothered you, one thing that you've never liked, one way in which you thought you were not the way that you should be, and use that as your starting point. You are no longer going to feel bad about that or spend time and energy trying to change it. You accept that it is what it is, and in this area of your life, at least, you will do whatever is the easiest, and then you get on with it.

Years ago, I had a roommate who was very handy and could do anything. She was always building bookshelves or reupholstering furniture, and when her bike broke, she took the whole thing apart and fixed it herself. I, on the other hand, could barely hang a poster on the wall (in fact, she often rehung them for me), and when my bike got a flat, it sat unridden for weeks. It was cost efficient and more self-sufficient to figure out how to change it myself, I kept thinking, all the while doing nothing about it. Then, finally, one day, I realized that I actually had no interest in learning how to fix it myself. It was totally okay for me to take it to the shop and pay someone else to fix it for me, because DIY bike maintenance was just not my thing.

Recently, my husband and I made the decision to downsize from our four-bedroom, hundred-plus-year-old house to a condo because, faced with both an endless list of home improvement projects and other things we'd rather be doing, we've come to the conclusion that home ownership is just not our thing. "We're not going to get a *Dwell* spread anytime soon," my husband said, and instead of feeling bad about that and spending our weekends arguing about whose turn it is to tackle the latest project, we're going to do what we need to do to make it easier on ourselves so that we can continue to focus on all the things that are, actually, *our thing*.

On the surface, it might seem like someone who loves and accepts themselves would be more prone to rejecting what comes into their lives, because they are sure of their worth and definitely don't want to settle for less. However, it's quite the opposite, in that the more you reject who you are to hold out for who you think you will be, the more you will reject circumstances, situations, people, and everything else that are also not what you think they should be. You'll end up rejecting anything that isn't exactly how you pictured it because you think that, unless you can get exactly what you want, you won't actually be worth anything. Who will you be if you can't make your dreams come true? Who will you be if you aren't able to get everything you want? Who will you be if you can't prove how much you are worth?

You'll be you. No matter how much you have, no matter how much you do, you will always be you. So make friends with yourself as you are now. Be nice to her. Allow her all her faults and flaws and fuckups, and then forgive her for them. Stop punishing yourself by rejecting the parts of you that you think aren't good enough. Stop denying yourself the experiences and emotions that don't fit in with who you think you should be. Embrace impermanence and change and growth and failure and loss and all the other inevitables because you know, truly know, that you can still love yourself. How well you fare in the storms, how well you will weather the transitions, how happy you will be, and how successful you will be all come down to being able to love yourself no matter what. Which, let's be honest, is a lot easier said than done.

But we can start. We can try. This is one area in our lives where we can try more instead of less. Instead of berating and criticizing and pushing and judging ourselves, we can try to work with what we have. We can try to be compassionate and kind and nurturing and understanding. All those gifts we have that we have spent our lives bestowing on other people, we can try to give a little bit of them to ourselves. We can try to remember, even in our darkest of times, that there is no better life for us than the one we have. There is no better way for us to be than the way we are. We often think that being rigid makes us strong, but the truth is that refusing to bend often just sets us up to break. We hold tight to the one vision that we have for ourselves and then find ourselves shattered by anything different. Snapping back from loss, disappointment, and heartbreak is a lot quicker when you're pliable.

I want to throw out some ideas that are very hard to accept, ideas that are counter to everything the inspirational clusterfuck wants you to believe, ideas that we have been taught to resist, ideas that will certainly make the haters lose their minds in the comments section. (Ha ha, joke's on you, haters! This is a book and there is no comment section!) But here they are:

Maybe you won't get everything you want.

Maybe no one does.

Maybe all your dreams won't come true.

Maybe you can accept that.

Maybe you can love yourself anyway.

## 13

## The Afternoon of My Life

I was in high school the first time I dyed my hair. It was 1995 and, like everyone else I knew, I'd seen *Pulp Fiction* about 7,562 times. So it was only natural that I wanted a Mia Wallace bob. My mom had always taken a laissez-faire approach to hair dyeing, so when my friend and I headed to the closest Osco in search of a box of black Clairol, my mom shrugged. I guess she figured teenagers had to make their own mistakes.

And mistake it was. Apply a box of black drugstore dye to naturally blond hair and you don't get black, and certainly not Mia Wallace midnight. What you get instead is an odd mix of green and purple, a strange color only ever seen intentionally on '90s cars like a Mitsubishi Eclipse or Dodge Neon. My friend and I stood in the bathroom of her older boyfriend's apartment, above the coffee shop where she worked, and surveyed the results. "It's . . . cute," she said.

"It's not exactly what I wanted," I admitted, but my approach to hair was even more laissez-faire than my mom's. For one, I didn't have the money for yet another box of dye, and for two, in this pre-internet era, we had no idea how to fix it. So I decided to do nothing. "I don't think anybody will notice," I said, and she agreed. We were wrong.

The next morning (just to clarify, I actually had a very supervised adolescence, in spite of dyeing my hair at an older guy's apartment on a school night), I had barely stepped foot in the hallway at school when it was practically a record screeching to a halt. Everybody noticed. "Oh my god, what did you do to your hair?" was the most common question I got, followed a close second by "Did you mean for it to look like that?" By third period, I had gotten tired of answering, "Tried to dye it," and "No," and wanted the day to hurry up and just end already so I could go home and immediately wash my head with Dawn dish soap, a suggestion kindly given to me by a teacher. I'll never forget an older girl in my math class, who had never been very nice, turning around in her seat and saying very earnestly, "I think it looks good." I mumbled a thanks, appreciating that she was genuinely trying to be kind, but also now miserably aware that my hair was so bad that it had inspired pity from someone who I was pretty sure didn't like me.

Later, after half a bottle of Dawn and multiple washings, my hair had acquired the texture of a hay bale but was still the color of a patinated penny, and as I pleaded through tears, my mom made me an appointment with a professional. A few days later, I sat in a salon chair, getting my first set of highlights, which returned me (almost) to pre-budget-Mia-Wallace normalcy. I've been dyeing my hair ever since.

At first, highlights were awesome, as they gave me summer hair all year round, and so I continued with them through high school and into college. When I worked as a beauty editor in New York, I got access to some of the city's best hairdressers who were willing to do my hair for free because their publicist told them it would be good for business (this was not totally accurate, as I had very little influence as an assistant). I took full advantage of this, though, and began experimenting beyond my usual repertoire. I became a redhead, a brunette, and once even got a perm (I loved it).

Around this time, in my midtwenties, I began to notice that in between the color switches, I had a few gray hairs. Far from panicking, though, I regarded them with curiosity, as gray hair was something that happened when you were older, and here I was, still young. I'd frequently show them to people, laugh about them, and blame them on my stressful NYC lifestyle (a joke at the time but in retrospect probably true).

Even though my gray hairs were multiplying, I didn't start to worry about them until I was in my early thirties, especially after my friend's uncle, who I'd just met, reached out and touched my temple and said, "Getting a little gray there, huh?" Now, this uncle was a noted asshole and later wore a MAGA hat to his niece's November 2016 wedding, but his comment, much like the girl in my math class so many years ago, alerted me to a bigger issue. If he was noticing, then other people were noticing, too. And I didn't want that.

Dyeing my hair ceased being an experiment or a way to play, and became a task, one that I undertook with a grim determination to tone, cover, and highlight those grays away. I'm still somewhat bitter about having to sit out the early 2010s ombre trend because I had to spend my hair-dye budget on my roots instead of my ends. I hadn't cared about my gray in my twenties, but now I wanted it gone. Because your thirties, that was a different story. Having gray hair meant that I was old.

Or did it? It certainly didn't feel like it, but the truth was, I didn't know. That was ten years ago. I've stopped dyeing my hair because there's too much gray to cover, but I still have no idea if I'm old. It turns out that growing up, and growing old, is mostly a gray area.

Society starts prepping us for becoming a grown-up pretty much from the time that we're born, and adulthood is often held out as either a threat or a promise. If we do what we're told and follow the rules, then adulthood is going to be glorious and full of wonderful things like having a job (!) and making car payments (!!). If we screw up too much, then we're certainly ruining not our present but our future, the time when we're supposed to be enjoying all the fruits of our laborious younger years. The constant question that we ask young people—*What do you want to be when you grow up?*—implies that they are nothing now and that *being* will happen sometime in the future, when they are older, with a career and a paycheck.

In spite of this belief that our childhood is little more than prep for being a grown-up, it's unclear when we actually become these grown-ups we've heard so much about. It's certainly not eighteen, when we can vote but are probably still in high school. It's also not twenty-one, when we can legally drink but still don't have a ton of life skills (I'd argue that the drinking actually works against the acquisition of life skills), and I doubt it's twenty-five, when we can finally rent a car, because renting a car isn't actually as much fun as it sounds. Maybe it's buying a house, or getting married, or becoming a parent, or ascending in your career, and yet I have done all of those things and still sometimes have trouble believing I'm not a kid anymore.

When we're young, we're led to believe that grown-ups have it all figured out. We're taught that grown-ups are rational, mature beings who always do the right thing. "Asparagus for dinner again," Laura Palmer wrote in her diary. "I hate asparagus. Does this mean I'll never grow up?" Sadly, as anyone who watched *Twin Peaks* could tell you, Laura did not grow up, but that had nothing to do with asparagus. But her pondering illustrates how so many of us have a hard time feeling grown up, or fully seeing ourselves as adults, when the adulthood narrative we've been sold doesn't fit us. We so rarely feel like we have anything, much less everything, figured out. We often feel like we're doing the wrong thing because we don't really know what the right thing is. A lot of the time, we still don't even really know who we are, and many of us are still waiting for the concrete identity that we were always told would arrive with age.

I was raised to respect authority and to see grown-ups as said authorities. I was taught that people who were older were automatically wiser, but my facepalm realization that age had little to do with maturity came soon after I started that first job as an assistant beauty editor. Part of my job was to catalog all the

free products that came into the office and set aside
the ones that we were going to photograph and write
about. My boss was fairly generous with giving away
the products that we weren't going to use, but one day,
a woman who worked on the ad sales side stopped by
my desk to let me know she'd spotted her favorite face
cream on one of our shelves and wanted to know if she
could have it.

I told her no, that we were planning to use that one
in a shoot, but she could probably have it if it came
back from the shoot in good shape (sometimes products were opened and scooped out or dribbled to mix
it up). She let me know how disappointed she was and
then stopped by my desk again, and again, asking first
if we still planned to use it, and later if it had been
shot yet. By the third time, I was annoyed and was
firm with her: yes, we were still planning on using it,
and the shoot we were saving it for wasn't scheduled
for several more weeks. Shortly after this, I looked over
at the shelf, and the face cream was gone.

I went running into my boss's office. "I think
Anne stole this moisturizer I wouldn't let her have,"
I blurted out, and much to my surprise, she wasn't
surprised. Instead, she sighed.

"Call the publicist and have them send over another one," she said.

"But she *stole* it!" I said.

"I'm sure she did," my boss said with an eye roll. "People steal stuff all the time. We might have to get a cabinet with a lock." I nodded and walked out of her office with my mind blown. Anne was high up on the ad sales team, probably making six figures, in her late forties, and she had just helped herself to something that someone had explicitly told her she could not have. She hadn't even been sneaky about it. I'd babysat toddlers with more shame.

I'm grateful to Anne, though, because I was only twenty-two when she taught me a lesson that proved invaluable throughout the rest of my career/life: adulthood is a myth. No one really knows what they're doing! Age does not always invite integrity, wisdom, or a closet full of sequined cocktail dresses (this last topic will be addressed in depth in my next book, tentatively titled *Eighties Movies Lied to Me*), and there is no magic number at which people become immune to doing immature stuff.

Grown-ups steal. They lie. They hurt others, sometimes without meaning to and sometimes on purpose. They do things that they know are wrong. We look around us and we see people who flounder and fail, make mistakes and question themselves. We see people who have ticked off all the boxes, hit all the major milestones, and still have no idea what the heck they are doing. Wouldn't it be great if we could all just admit that this is the norm and not the exception? Instead, we spend a lot of time cataloging others' mistakes and missteps, comparing ourselves to them, and beating ourselves up for our own mistakes and missteps, which we think have derailed our grown-up trajectory. We end up with ideas about where we should be at certain ages and what we think we should have accomplished, and when we don't manage to hit these mile markers, we feel like we have failed. *Everyone else has it all figured out*, you tell yourself— you're the only one struggling. This is a lie, though, and the truth is that almost everyone, in some way or another, is on plan b (or plan c, d, e, or f).

One beautiful fall day, not too long ago, I was in a great mood, so I decided to ruin it by going on Instagram. One of the first posts I saw was from another author whose debut YA novel had come out in 2019, the same year as mine. Also like mine, her debut had been the first book in a trilogy, but unlike mine, all three of her books had become bestsellers. She now had close to fifty thousand followers, and because I was one of them, I knew that she also had three young children. She was posting about her birthday and how grateful she was to be surrounded by so much love from her family and her fans.

She had just turned twenty-eight.

Twenty-fucking-eight??? She had three kids and

three bestsellers by twenty-eight? I spent my twenty-eighth birthday eating Papa John's and playing *Guitar Hero*, and I threw up later that night, not from drinking but from topping off all that garlic butter sauce with four vegan cupcakes and a tofu dog. I wasn't even vegan! Later that year, I moved from New York to Philadelphia because I figured *packing up everything I owned and restarting my life in a new city* was easier than actually breaking up with my boyfriend (never been a fan of confrontation). At twenty-eight, the only creature I took care of was a hand-me-down fish named Bill—and Bill died. I didn't even take care of myself (see above re: cupcakes). At twenty-eight, I sucked. The more I ruminated on this, the more I decided that I didn't just suck at twenty-eight, that I also sucked now. That other woman had done everything right, probably from the time she was born, whereas I'd spent years struggling and falling behind and life had passed me by and now I was too old to even dream of catching up.

When I was still trying to have another baby, this was a line of thinking that I frequently revisited. I spent a lot of time and energy being mad at my younger self for the decisions that she made because I assumed that if she had done differently, then I would not have found myself where I was, which was in my forties and feeling like a failure because I desperately wanted something that I wasn't going to get. This was classic self-blame as self-soothing, but it also wasn't fair to my younger self. Sure, she was a little messy, but overall, she had actually created the life she wanted for herself. When I was young, the only thing I knew for certain was that I didn't want my life to be boring. I wanted to travel, read a lot of books and write a few of them, live in big cities and know interesting people, and I'd done all of that. Looking at myself through my teenage eyes, it seemed like that girl would see her future and be stoked about it. It wasn't fair to look back at my younger self and wish that she had been someone completely different. If she'd been completely different, then I would be, too, and frankly, I'm tired of thinking that there's nothing about myself that couldn't do with being tossed in the trash.

Asking successful people (women, especially) what advice they would give to their younger selves is a very popular interview question, but really, what's the point? There is no golden nugget of wisdom that would have saved us from heartbreak or failure, that would have changed our trajectory and landed us someplace "better." This is just another way of wishing we were someone else, someplace else, doing something else, another tactic that keeps us from enjoying who and where we are. This is another way that we reject ourselves and our experiences and withhold self-acceptance because of a past that is entirely unchange-able in the present. If I had a time machine, the only thing I would want to tell my younger self is to stop plucking her eyebrows, because they do not grow back. I would also tell her that she is doing a great job, and to be proud of herself because, as it were, my younger self got plenty of advice and admonishment and far too little affirmation.

Age is one area of our life where our shoulds be-come an impossible-to-navigate maze of unwritten rules. I doubt I'm the only one who spent much of my life thinking I was too young to live how I really wanted, only to have that feeling flip one day. Suddenly, the reason that I couldn't live how I really wanted was that now I was too old. From the time we're kids, we're told to act our age, even though what that means is often defined as what is most beneficial to the person telling us to do so. You can be told "You're not a kid anymore" when someone wants you to do something, yet also be told "You're not a grown-up" when that same person doesn't want you to do something. We are rarely allowed to define age appropriateness for our-selves and instead consistently smack up against things that might have felt right to us only to be told that oh, no, no, that is so wrong! You thought you looked cute, but you cannot wear a shirt like that at your age!

*Age appropriate* is so often treated like something

that is concrete, when maturity levels only occasionally correlate with age (shout-out to Anne from ad sales) and what is appropriate for one person at fifteen might still not be appropriate for someone else at twenty-five. Also, more often than not, age appropriateness becomes another vehicle for keeping us locked in patterns of trying to be how and who we think we should be rather than letting ourselves truly be who we are. We spend much of our youth trying to look and seem older and much of our adulthood trying to look younger. Once again, we're never allowed to simply be. We're always either too young or too old, and never just right.

Teenage girls are a prime example of this impossible set of expectations. They're sexualized for their youth while dismissed because of it. This was an issue that I ran into as a YA author; it was assumed that writing a book meant for teenage girls must not have been as hard as writing a book for, you know, like, real people. Ideas that are embraced and championed by young women are automatically written off as frivolous, even when those ideas support billion-dollar industries. I know this is a matter of personal preference, but I've always taken umbrage with the belief that it's trivializing to call women "girls" because that assumes that girls are trivial. It's the opposite. If girls weren't so powerful, then the patriarchy wouldn't bother spending so much time and effort trying to convince us otherwise.

Most of what we have been told about aging is a lie. You can still be attractive at any age. You can still pursue goals, find love, change your life, start something entirely new. At whatever age you are, you can do almost anything you want. However, the "almost" here can be hard to accept and often feels unfair. I remember once walking into work in my late twenties to find the fashion editor sitting at her desk, staring off into space and looking particularly despondent. When I asked her what was wrong, she sighed. "I just realized I will never be a teen idol," she said. "I mean, why wasn't my mom a stage mom?"

The awareness of this winnowing can hit like a slap in the face, especially when it comes to fertility. When you hear generalized discussion of women like me, who went to begin families in their late thirties or early forties only to be hit with challenge after challenge, these women are often written off as having "waited too long." They're profiled as now paying the price for having spent too much time dedicated to their careers. This would suggest that such women were surrounded by eligible suitors dying to impregnate them and were instead like, "No, I can't have a baby now because I have to send these emails!"

I don't know anyone like this. Instead, I know lots of women who followed the program and who tried, very hard, to do everything right. I was the recipient (er, victim?) of 1990s public school sex education, which involved wall-size color projections of STDs and stressed, over and over, how having a baby before you were 110 percent ready would absolutely ruin your life and the lives of everyone around you. So all those years that I wasted waiting too long, I was trying to get myself to that 110 percent. I wanted to wait for the right guy and also make sure that I could support myself and a child if that right guy somehow turned out to be the wrong one, and I wanted to make sure that I had enough life experience and personal growth behind me so that I wouldn't someday freak out and leave my family behind to hit the road as a groupie for a Grateful Dead cover band. Sure, I always heard that fertility declines after thirty-five, but this was contrary to what I'd also always heard, about how important it was to wait and be totally ready. So, between those two choices, I did what I always did and went with what seemed like the less risky option because I was a good girl, and that was what I had always been taught to do. The joke, I guess, was on me.

In Sheila Heti's novel *Motherhood*, the main character ruminates on whether or not she should have children in her late thirties and ultimately decides not to. "I am in the afternoon of my life," she writes. "The time for children is breakfast." I thought about this quote a lot when I was deciding how hard I wanted to pursue getting pregnant. As time dragged on without success, I realized that I didn't really want pancakes for dinner. Meaning, I didn't really want to have another baby at this stage in my life—what I wanted was to have already had it, when I was younger, when things were different. Admitting this to myself made it a little easier to let go. We can become so committed to the pursuit that sometimes we continue to chase a dream that, if we give ourselves the time and space and honesty to examine it, isn't really our dream anymore. Walking away from those goals is growing up, not giving up.

For millennial women, the pandemic threw an extra wrench in the works when it came to the passage of time and aging, because it arrived when many of us felt like life was really getting going. We were well into adulthood, but not yet old, and we were starting to feel like the life that we had always wanted, the life that we'd really been working for, was finally in sight. And then, boom. We left the workforce in droves, did what had to be done, and then when we were ready to come back, we found that it wasn't so easy to pick up right where we'd left off. The world had changed, entire industries had changed. Everything was all about how Gen Z was coming to get theirs, and we felt stunned, because we still hadn't gotten ours. It seemed like only yesterday we were the up-and-comers, and now we were being shown the glass door when we'd been expecting to smash the glass ceiling. It feels like reading a book where someone has ripped out a couple of chapters from the middle, and as a former intern of mine (who's now in her midforties and owns her own company, because we're that old) said, "Wait, but where are my millions?!"

So, here we are, juggling the fact that a lot of what we expected to happen didn't, a lot of stuff that we never saw coming did, we've got too much to do, things hurt in ways they didn't used to, we've got gray hair and wrinkles and still the occasional zit, and it's all just so WTF! So, what do we do now? Certainly not a midlife crisis, because that's too cliché and honestly, our bank accounts probably won't allow for convertibles and our schedules won't allow for affairs with our tennis instructors (in fact, our schedules probably haven't allowed for tennis lessons in the first place).

But what about a midlife awakening? A big, seismic shift in our lives that isn't so much a breakdown as it is a breakout. What if we use midlife as a time to truly, for the first time ever, dedicate ourselves to ourselves? Age appropriateness be damned, once and for all, because at the end of the day, aging is a wonderful thing that means you are not dead yet! And it means that you are, without a doubt, a grown-up, even if you don't like asparagus. This is glorious because it means that you are in charge of you. You are the boss! You make the decisions! You really, truly do. So how do you want to live your life?

For me, one of the few things I know for sure is that I do not want to live the second half of my life in the same way I lived my first. I have spent so much time trying to make myself small. I tried to fit into the little space that was allocated for me. I have worried excessively about offending anyone or making people uncomfortable. I prioritized other people liking me over me liking myself. I strove for approval and permission in everything I did and went above and beyond trying to earn it. I played by all the rules. I did everything that was expected of me and more. I tried so hard to prove myself, to earn my happiness and joy and self-worth. To make everyone else happy. I tried, so hard, to be good. But now, I'm too old for that shit.

I don't know that I've ever been so excited about my future as I am now, in my midforties. Sure, I was excited when I was younger, but I was also scared. I was scared I'd mess it up, that I wasn't good enough to get what I wanted, that I wouldn't be able to hold on tight enough to keep life from passing me by. I'm not scared anymore, because I no longer believe the world when it tries to tell me I am getting it all wrong. I know what I am doing—which is whatever the fuck I want.

When our parents' generation turned forty, they

broke out the tombstone-shaped sheet cake and threw "Over the Hill" parties, an idea that surely makes us balk now. But what if we're not so much over the hill as we are over the hump, and it's not going to be such an uphill battle anymore? Maybe life is downhill from here, not in a going-to-hell way, but in a way that just means we don't have to pedal so hard all the time. We can cruise a little bit, and when we hit a bump we can know that we're not going to crash. We might even fly.

# 14

## Girls Just Want to Have Friends

The morning after Star—one of my two best friends—died, I was on the phone with a psychic. This was not planned but a coincidence, as I was in the middle of researching a magazine story on celebrities' favorite fortune tellers, and this guy was apparently Jennifer Lopez's go-to.

I told him that my best friend had died just a few hours before. He explained that he might not be able to locate her, since so little time had elapsed, but he paused and soon had a question. "Would your friend be showing me Boston?" he asked, explaining that he was getting messages from someone who wanted to talk to me about Boston.

"No," I said, disappointed. Neither Star nor I had ever lived there, had no connection. He and I talked for a little longer, but there was nothing revelatory, and when I hung up, I had the feeling that he was mostly full of shit.

Star and I met in college in Kansas. We weren't close, but we had mutual friends and knew each other well enough that she offered up her couch, in her south Williamsburg apartment, when she heard I was moving to New York. The "couch" turned out to be a repurposed van seat, but the week that I spent sleeping on it cemented Star's and my friendship to the point where, a little over a year later, we found ourselves roommates, this time in a much bigger apartment in Greenpoint and with furniture that had not been made by Ford.

She was working as a chef at the time, both in restaurants and for private clients, and I was a low-level magazine editor writing freelance on the side. In short, we hustled and supported each other through the ups and downs of a life with long hours and little money. But our existence was far from a slog, and Star and I both lived with a certain joie de vivre that was, I think, unique to Kansas girls who found themselves in the Big City. She howled with laughter when it turned out that my brand-new A.P.C. raw denim jeans (a major splurge) were so stiff and tight that I couldn't squat down enough to get into a taxi and so had to crawl in headfirst. When her private clients let her borrow their car, she immediately picked me up so that we could hit the McDonald's drive-through for fries and a fountain Coke and cruise Williamsburg's Bedford Avenue while blasting HOT 97. When I bawled my eyes out in the bathtub over a guy who wasn't worth it, I got out to find she'd left a note of encouragement on my bed.

Eventually, I left New York for Philadelphia, and Star for Portland, Oregon, and a career in the wine industry. Despite our distance, we never grew apart or lost touch. We managed to see each other several times a year and spoke frequently on the phone. Sometimes, we'd find out that we were reading the same book, or had been listening to the same music, or had both just fixed ourselves a Negroni before we decided to pick up the phone.

Star was a sommelier and a gourmand who didn't turn up her nose at a PBR and who made me pigs in a blanket when I was eight months pregnant. She had fiery red hair and complained that whenever you saw a picture of a redhead, they were always dressed like they were headed to a Renaissance faire. I laughed her off until she made me look up red hair on Wikipedia, and I saw that she was right. When my son was born a redhead, she sent him a baby blanket with owls on it and a note that said, "I just know we are going to be best friends."

Star didn't have kids of her own, but she was the

kind of grown-up who could easily be friends with a child, and I liked to imagine how her prophecy would come true. Maybe summer trips to apprentice with Aunt Star, learning to stomp grapes and tow the chicken tractor through the vineyards, and then sitting shotgun while she barreled through wine country, dispensing the kind of quips she was famous for, Starisms like "Freelance means eating salad in your car."

She and the baby got to meet on his first Thanksgiving, when we traveled to Portland to spend it with her and a few other friends. It was a cozy meal, with delicious food and, thanks to Star, plentiful good wine, and then, a month later, she was diagnosed with cancer. We were all optimistic about how things would work out. She started shopping for head wraps, I started stocking up on books that I thought she'd like, and we made plans for me to come up so that I could help her through one of the treatments. At this point, we'd known each other for twenty years, and I imagined how we'd look back on all of this in twenty more. I knew it was going to change her life forever.

Her first round of chemo was hard, and instead of recovering after it, she got worse. I remember the confusion in those days, mass emails with updates from friends who were medical professionals, finally reporting that she was going to be hospitalized. I flew up to surprise her and waited until my plane had landed to call. "Hey," I said, when she answered, "I'm in Portland. You need a visitor?" After a few seconds of disbelief, she was excited, and I asked if I could bring her anything.

"Nutritious, delicious food," she said. "You know what I like!" I took an Uber from the airport to the fancy grocery store, bought her just that, and then headed to the hospital. When I found her room, the door was closed. I knocked and waved, brandishing my bag of groceries, only to have a woman I didn't recognize motion at me to wait in the hall. A few minutes later, a friend came out and explained that had been the hospital's head of palliative care, who was just informing Star that they were recommending she receive no further treatment and be released into hospice instead.

It was winter in Oregon that day, and snow started to swirl down outside the hospital windows as I sat with Star and the day turned into night. She couldn't really eat the nutritious, delicious food I had brought, but she tried, and she still asked me questions. How was my book coming along? How was my son? Had I been to any good restaurants recently? Where had we stayed when we'd gone to Mexico City? I played her a Weezer cover of Black Sabbath from my phone, and she asked me to please turn it off (what was I thinking?). We watched a movie, and I let her pick, without arguing for once. Star and I shared many similar interests, but movies were not one of them. She liked documentaries and stark dramas, whereas I liked films with long shopping montages or chase scenes. As roommates in the early 2000s, I'd been the first to get a Netflix account, back when they still sent DVDs in the mail. She'd opened the first red envelope that arrived at our apartment, and texted me, "You signed up for Netflix and the first thing you rent is *Beverly Hills Cop*?"

"Watch it with me or sit in your room," I wrote back, though in the end, of course, she couldn't resist Eddie Murphy.

The movie she chose that night in the hospital was predictably grim, about a homeless man and his daughter being forcibly reintegrated into society, but I gritted my teeth and sat through it. "Do you hate it?" she asked. "Mostly," I said, and we watched it till the end.

The next morning, before I flew back home, I went back to the hospital. "I love you, and I'll see you again soon," I said before I left, but it turned out that I would not.

A few weeks after her death, I was going through old voicemails. Like many people, I don't actually listen to them, and as it was, I had several from Star that I had never played before. I sat on my bed, listening to them before emailing them to myself to save. In one, she was laughing. "I love that you don't have your voicemail set up," she said about the fact that it still just said the number, and not my name, even though I'd had the same number for almost twenty years. "Don't ever change," she said. "And call me back. Even though I know you won't listen to this." That was when the enormity of her death washed over me. I'd lost someone who really, truly knew me, and loved me anyway. Then I remembered Boston.

I'd been living in New York for a couple of months, in an apartment I'd found on Craigslist, when Star asked if I wanted to go with her to visit one of her friends from college, now living in Boston. I jumped at the chance and told her I knew just how we'd get there. I'd taken the Chinatown bus once before, which got me from New York to Boston for ten dollars, and explained to Star how it was so easy and cheap and we should definitely do that.

I bought our tickets, and on a warm fall night, we met in Chinatown to board the bus. The bus that I had taken previously had actually been pretty nice, but the one we were boarding now was a different story. It was a short bus, with no bathroom, and it smelled. Traffic was heavy on a Friday evening, and what had been a four-hour trip for me before was now stretching into six, seven hours, especially as the bus made periodic stops along the way at Chinese restaurants so that everyone could get out to use the restroom. Our emotions cycled from frustration to anger to despair to hunger and finally, giddy acceptance. "How is it taking so long when we're going so fast?" Star pondered. "I feel like we're flying down the highway in a tuna can."

"This is nothing," said the girl in the seat next to us. "Last time I took this bus, the door broke and the driver took his shirt off to tie it shut. It kept flapping open, and snow would blow down the aisle." Star and I laughed so hard we couldn't breathe. Fung Wah Bus Transportation was eventually shut down after the US Department of Transportation deemed it an "imminent hazard to public safety," but I will be forever grateful for it, because that tuna can to Boston cemented a close friendship that was a pillar of my life for the next sixteen years. Maybe Jennifer Lopez's psychic wasn't so full of shit after all.

If you were to glean your cues about what it takes to live a good life from books, movies, TV shows, and songs—and, let's face it, many of us do—you would come away believing that love was the most important and defining thing in a woman's life. But not just any kind of love—romantic love. This is the kind of love where a prince makes it his mission to sweep you off your feet, the kind of love where a vampire declares that you are what he's spent centuries searching for, the kind of love where a superhot billionaire bad boy wants to be good just for you. This, we are told, is the most important kind of love. The love that we should seek, the love that we should hold out for, the love that will set us free and make us whole and teach us who we really are.

I beg to differ. Yeah, sex is cool, but have you ever had a female friend love and support you unconditionally? That's a love worth seeking.

Star and I became best friends at twenty-two, but before that, I met my other best friend when we were eighteen and living in the same dorm our freshman year of college. We'd seen each other around but never really hung out until we found ourselves at a house party on 4/20, which everyone at our predominantly white college celebrated as "Bob Marley's birthday" (which is actually February 6). The party involved a DJ poorly mixing Bob Marley song with Bob Marley song, lots of wall-hung tapestries, and bowls full of joints. The dirty bare feet were numerous and the weed/BO/patchouli haze was nauseating and when she said, "I'm walking home," I said, "I'll come with you." From that day forward, we were best friends, and a few years later, she graced me with one of the most powerful and life-changing acts of unconditional love that I have ever experienced. In probably the single worst act of my entire life, I made out with her ex-boyfriend going into our junior year of college, and when he told her, instead of never speaking to me again (as she had every right to do), she was concerned. "What is wrong with you?" she asked.

I thought I knew what was wrong with me and that I was just a horrible person. Instead, it turned out that I was depressed. I wouldn't figure that out for another decade or so, though, and her refusal to give up on me then, or any other time in our now twenty-five-year friendship, has been one of the primary reasons I never fully gave up on myself.

I love my husband immensely, and at this point, we have been together for ten years, but I met him when I was thirty-four. I've done plenty of growing in the past decade, but when we met, I'd already smoothed out a lot of my rough edges and my act was pretty much together. He has never seen me blackout drunk from bottomless mimosa brunch, or stressed because I've maxed out my credit card cash withdrawal limit and so can't pay my rent. He didn't have to still go places with me when I was in my poncho phase, and I never bought him a juice cleanse from Groupon and then insisted we do it together. By the time we met, I'd learned to keep my car clean. He's also, at this point, not so interested in hearing me rehash the same situations I've rehashed nine hundred times before. My best friend, on the other hand, will still answer a call from me in the middle of her workday because I just saw Kourtney Kardashian's pregnancy announcement and have started to cry.

No one would argue that romantic love doesn't feel good, but the reason that it occupies such a central role in what we think it takes to live a successful life is because, once again, our patriarchal society has conditioned us to think this way. If we think that the most important thing in our life is our ability to have a relationship with a man, then we will go to great lengths to sustain those relationships. We will attempt to sustain those relationships even at great peril to our own happiness and well-being. We will let men determine our worth, we will go out of our way to mold ourselves into what pleases them, and we will never stop trying to win their approval. You know, we'll do all that shit that we've been doing!

On the contrary, if we were taught to view our female friends as our true partners in building the lives we want to live and becoming the people we want to become, then we'd be much less likely to put up with all of that stuff that wears us down. So, instead, we're taught that female friendships are rife with backstabbing and drama. We're exposed to countless narratives about how women are catty and competitive, and we learn that women can't really be trusted.

Ironically, though, one of the most harmful narratives

that we're fed about female friendship is that, if you are lucky enough to find a ride-or-die best friend, this relationship requires very little effort. It should sustain itself. Your relationship with your romantic partner will take work, and there will be ups and downs, we are taught, but it should be totally different with your best friend. It's no big deal if you don't call your best friend back for weeks on end, or cancel plans because something better came up. She's your best friend— she'll understand! Female friendship is yet another area of our lives where we have been taught to expect perfection and then write the whole damn thing off as worthless the minute it falls short. And it will fall short, especially if you put zero effort in.

But when you do put effort in, you will almost certainly be rewarded. Of course, women are human, and over a lifetime of friendships, you will run into people who are not worth the effort; those "friends" tend to weed themselves out. But the ones who respond in kind, with effort of their own, often go on to become the friends who enrich your life and make it better in every way.

So many of us are at this point in our lives where we're realizing that everything we've been taught is a lie, the futures we've been working for don't exist, and the institutions we swore allegiance to and have been working for don't really give a crap about us. So where do we go from here? What do we do now? What we do is double down on our female friendships. This life is crazy, this world is crazy, and the only way we are going to get through it is together.

Research has shown that the female stress response is not as much "fight or flight," which places a high emphasis on the individual, as it is "tend and befriend." Women respond to stress by nurturing those in their care and reducing risk by becoming affiliated with social groups, and then using these groups—and particularly their relationships with other females—to better manage stressful conditions. I think we've reached a critical point where we must tend and befriend like never before. We must tend to those we love, ourselves included, and continue to expand our networks, not in a "let's connect on LinkedIn" kind of way but in a true "I got you and you got me" kind of way. We have to build community in our day-to-day lives, and that's hard to do when you are booked and scheduled to the hilt.

Not too long after we moved back to Kansas, we joined a community pool, and I remember being there one afternoon and watching a group of women with interest. There were about six or seven of them, standing in the shallow end chatting, and they were all passing around a baby, taking turns bouncing and holding it, all except for one woman, who mostly sat on the side of the pool sipping a frozé. After watching for a while, I realized that this woman was the baby's mother, and her friends were gifting her something invaluable to new moms: the chance to be in charge of only your own body for a while. I watched as someone, not the mom, changed a diaper, and then another rocked the stroller when the baby needed a nap. When the mother and the baby finally left, someone even helped her carry all her stuff out to her car. *Wow*, I thought. *If I'd had that, maybe I wouldn't have ended up so depressed.*

In the years prior to getting pregnant, I had been focused on writing my first novel. I was freelance at the time, but still had a slate of full-time client work, so the sacrifice I made for my own writing was my social life. I skipped a lot of parties and brunches in order to stay home with my computer. I thought my social life was extraneous, but I was wrong. Friendships and community both require consistency—you cannot value them only when you need them. You must value them when others need them as well. This might seem contrary to everything else I've said in this book ("But you've been saying to do less, not more! I'm supposed to put myself first!"), but being a good friend is, I think, one of the ultimate acts of self-care.

Our modern lives are set up as if we're walking a tightrope. We think we're not alone, because we can look around and see so many people we know also walking their own individual tightropes. But when one of us falls, we're all so busy trying to maintain our own balance (and not look down!) that we can't do anything to help. I don't want the tightrope anymore. I want a wide, flat bridge, something I can leisurely stroll across arm in arm with all the other women who happen to be heading my way. I want a safety net. I want to be the safety net, because it's so much easier to bounce back when you have people who never let you actually hit the ground.

## 15

## Here Comes the Sun

The '90s were a great time to be a teenage witch. Metaphysical shops were everywhere, you could buy candles adorned with suns and moons and yin-yang symbols from kiosks at the mall, and *The Craft* hit theaters on my sixteenth birthday. I decorated my bedroom walls with images of gods and goddesses I bought from Spencer's Gifts, hotboxed with nag champa, and attempted many things that I thought might bring me enlightenment, like once trying to smoke peppermint tea by rolling it up in a Post-it. I'd camp out on the floor of the astrology section of Borders Books & Music, looking up everyone I knew in *The Secret Language of Birthdays*, and used my babysitting money to buy a deck of tarot cards. I also proudly declared myself an atheist to anyone who would listen. Witchcraft was one thing. God, with his beige churches and judgmental followers, something else.

For most of my life, this pretty much summed up my spiritual beliefs. I had a vague sense that I was looking for something, a sort of knowing that might finally allow me to relax, but for the most part, I saw this pursuit as entertainment, the aesthetic dabbling of someone who'd grown up with *Buffy the Vampire Slayer* and Winona Ryder movies. I never quite managed to believe in the magic that I played around with, and I didn't believe in anything else, either.

In fact, I tended to look down on belief in general. It seemed like a cop-out to me. When I'd hear people say things like "God has a plan for me," I'd mentally roll my eyes. They must just not have worked hard enough, I always thought. People who believed in a higher power were lazy and looking for excuses for why they hadn't been able, or willing, to do whatever it takes. I knew that happiness, success, fulfillment— everything, really—was up to each individual person and how hard they were willing to try to get it. When it came to making things happen in my life, I believed that there were only three forces at play: me, myself, and I. To pretend otherwise was letting myself off the hook and, no matter what, I was not going to let myself off the hook. It was all on me. Everything in my life was because of me. Everything came down to what I did or did not do. Me, me, me.

It took feeling pretty damn powerless to change my mind. For me, this came in 2020. Fresh off a miscarriage and an emergency surgery, in a pandemic with a toddler, and I was one of the lucky ones because we actually still had, for the most part, our health. I was so used to having agency, to coming up with a plan and then throwing myself wholeheartedly into seeing that plan through, and now I couldn't even meet a friend for coffee. I started to think that maybe there was a plan bigger than my plan, though that didn't mean that I had to like it. Or that it was even a good plan. As Denise says in the emotional climax of that cinematic classic *Can't Hardly Wait*, "You know, judging from my little experience, I kind of believe in fate. It just works in really fucked-up ways sometimes."

That spring and summer, I went on lots of walks, because it was one of the only things I could do that felt like doing something. With my son in the stroller, some days we'd walk seven or eight miles, and if seen from above, I'm sure our trajectory would have looked like Billy's from *Family Circus*: loops and lines that crisscrossed and dissected themselves, treading the same territory over and over and ultimately going nowhere fast.

But it didn't feel like that. In fact, as I walked and

tried to make sense of these uncertain times, on a personal and global level, it felt like I was finally getting somewhere. I was starting to see a glimmer of something that felt both hopeful and scary. It hinted at the idea that I had to stop trying so hard to control everything, because I wasn't actually in control. My life wasn't just about me, and if I could believe in the idea of a force bigger than myself, then I could let go a little bit. I could stop trying to do it all.

That summer, I started meditating. It was nothing fancy, just sitting by the water or under a tree for a few minutes, closing my eyes and making a conscious effort to listen to the sounds of the birds and the waves and the leaves rather than running through to-do lists or making plans. It was an effort to slow down, to align my screeching, speeding interior with the pace of nature, and the more I did it, the more I began to realize that I'd gone most of my life without ever really paying attention to my thoughts.

Sure, I was always thinking, and usually overthinking. About goals, responsibilities, worries, comparisons, judgments, other people. But this was all small stuff that kept me preoccupied with doing and left little room for considering the big stuff. You know, like who was I? Why was I here? What did I really want? What did I believe in?

I'd love to say that I had some sort of spiritual

awakening, but in reality, I pretty much made the decision to believe in a higher power because I figured, hell, why not? In some ways, it seemed like the one thing I hadn't tried. As time dragged on and I kept losing pregnancies, I'd find myself panicking about how I was going to control and organize and effort my way into another baby, spiraling about possibilities and everything there was to do. How was I going to do everything right and not make mistakes and take care of everyone and maximize joy and minimize hurt and make enough money and sanitize all the hands and not just totally lose my mind in the process when there was so much riding on every single decision I had to make?

The only thing that would pull me out of these tailspins was taking a deep breath and acknowledging that there might be forces greater than I could even imagine at play here. After a lifetime of taking on more work than I could really handle, it felt incredibly freeing and hopeful to hand over some of that responsibility to something else, even if I wasn't sure what that something else was.

So maybe that is a cop-out. Maybe believing in something bigger than yourself is a form of cope, a way of making yourself feel not so bad when things get tough. But what's wrong with occasional cope? What is wrong with believing in something that makes you feel better? I don't think everything has to be so hard all the time, and believing that it's not all on you does make it easier. Cosmically, I'm an infinitesimal speck. An infinitesimal speck that's strong as fuck, but a speck nonetheless, and specks can only hold so much. I eventually got to the point where I had to believe in something bigger or collapse under the weight of everything I was trying to hold on my own.

You can't just white-knuckle it and will your way into the life that is meant for you, into a life that will truly make you happy and bring you inner peace. If all it really took to get what you wanted out of life was being willing to work for it, then we'd all have it by now. Happiness, fulfillment, love, joy—all the things that really make life worth living aren't about control, work, or trying. They're about surrender, about letting go and giving in to the idea that everything is connected, that every little thing is a source of wonder. Even you.

When we come across a young person who is having a hard time, we love to tell them, "It gets better." This is a lie. The truth is, the more you progress in your life, the more you grow, the more you love, the more you succeed, the more you are able to craft your life into the life that you want, the worse it gets. Why? Because it gets scarier. Because the more you love, the more you have to lose. The more you lead with your heart, the harder the hurts hit. Honestly, I'm amazed that we all still get out of bed in the morning, because holy shit, having a life that you love is terrifying! But it is the only way to go. The fear is worth it, and you owe it to yourself to take the risks and make the changes, big and small, that you need to get there. Call it *cope* if you want, but I do believe that there is a grand plan for each and every one of us. It's up to us, though, to be brave enough to follow it.

Death is the ultimate life hack, and nothing puts things in perspective like remembering that you are going to die. Everyone you love is going to die. We hope and pray that it's years from now at a ripe old age, but the truth is that we never know. It could be next week, tomorrow, or even later today. So, if there is any takeaway from the chaos of the last few years, let it be that life is indeed wild and precious. How do you want to spend yours? What is the meaning of your life? Who are you? What were you put on this planet to do? I don't think it's just the dishes.

No one is going to give us the time and space to think about the big stuff; we're just going to have to take it, because it's really hard to find your purpose when you're bogged down. When you spend so much time doing all the things you're told you should do, you don't have much time left over for the things you really want to do. That, right there, is why it's so important to stop trying. When you stop trying, you pull your energy and time and power back from the million vampires that are sucking it up at all cost and no benefit to you. You bring it back to yourself and use it to create a life that really makes you feel alive. This is different from "the life of your dreams," where you have everything you've ever wanted and where everything looks just like how you think it should look. This is a life where you feel like you are truly yourself, you are worthy, and, no matter what happens, you are who you were meant to be and doing what you were meant to do.

It's hard to fully live your life when you're so stressed you can't sleep, so exhausted you can't think, spread thin trying to please everyone, and so busy you can't even remember the last time you had the space to have a thought that was bigger than "chicken nuggets." We're all here to make a difference, in some way, somehow, for someone. It's mission critical at this point, because if anyone is going to save the world—and this place needs to be saved—it's going to be women. Women who have stopped trying to do everything so that they can do what actually matters, what makes a difference.

So, just to recap, here's how we stop trying: We learn to quit. We recognize our own misogyny and stop judging. We put ourselves first sometimes. We tend to our mental health. We don't stay positive. We listen to our intuition. We overachieve because we want to, not because we have to. We recognize that sometimes, things just don't work out. We de-emphasize productivity and reduce overscheduling. We counter our worries. We practice acceptance. We let go of our shoulds. We big-up ourselves. We value our friends, and we believe in something bigger than a speck.

I still have that same deck of tarot cards I bought with my babysitting money, and as part of my meditation practice a few years ago, I began to draw one every day. Each of the seventy-eight cards represents a different idea or characteristic, and more often than not, interpreting the cards will lead you to probe deeper into something that you probably already know. As my quest to have another baby dragged on and the disappointments mounted, I began to cling to the tarot cards because I needed them to tell me there was still hope.

On my third and final round of IUI, I was sure there was hope. I had science on my side, after all, and an ultrasound had revealed that I had two eggs ready to go, just about as good as I could hope for. After the procedure, I found myself growing more and more hopeful. I wasn't supposed to take a pregnancy test for two weeks, though, to reduce the chances of a false negative, so I counted down the days. On the night of the thirteenth day, I was excited because I was almost sure that the next morning we'd get the news we'd been waiting for. As I shuffled my tarot cards, a thought flitted through my mind: *If I draw the sun, then this baby is for sure gonna happen.* (If you're not familiar with tarot cards, the image on the sun is of a cherubic toddler riding on the back of a horse in a blaze of bright and happy glory. It is a card of hope and good things to come.)

I took a deep breath, cut the cards, and pulled one. It wasn't the sun. I don't remember what it was, because it was so disappointing, I didn't even bother to write it down.

The next morning, I woke early and went straight to the bathroom to take a pregnancy test. It was negative, and I was stunned. Later that morning, I went for a walk. It was early spring, sunny but still with a damp chill in the air. The ground was a little wet and muddy, and sunlight filtered down through the trees, speckling the ground with shadows of branches that were starting to bud. I walked into the woods for a fair bit, and when I came across a large fallen tree trunk, I sat on it to meditate. I set a timer, closed my eyes, and tried to focus on all the sounds that were around me, just as I always did. When the timer finally dinged the most melodic chime I could find on my iPhone, I opened them again. I took a few deep breaths and looked around, and through the trees, across the path and up against a log, I saw something that I didn't notice when I sat down. I couldn't quite tell what it was, but it was interesting, so I decided to walk closer, even though I warned myself not to get my hopes up. I grew up reading stories of magical discoveries—portals and amulets and jewels—and now, as an author, I write them, but I know how rare such discoveries are in real life. Get close enough and most treasure turns out to be trash.

But this time, when I picked my way through the dead leaves and sticks, I couldn't believe what I saw. It was a little woven basket, the handle fraying, and inside was a deck of tarot cards peeking out from a leather case. I could tell that the cards were well loved and that they hadn't just fallen out of a pocket or been left behind. Someone had put them there, deliberately, for reasons I'll never know, maybe for someone else to find. The card on top, plainly visible, was the sun.

I was so stunned that I actually looked around me for someone who had put them there, for someone who was playing a joke, but aside from the birds and a couple of squirrels, I was alone. At first, I interpreted that card of warmth and light and optimism as a sign that all my trying was going to pay off. Now, though, I look back and think that it was telling me that I was going to be okay even if it didn't.

That, ultimately, is what I hope you'll take from

this book: The next time you're confronted with a situation where you're tempted to try, try again—because that's what you've always done—you can instead trust. You can trust that your life is still a work of art, even if it ends up looking nothing like the picture you had painted in your head. You can trust that you know what's best for you, even when someone else is saying that you don't. You can trust that everything's not going to fall apart the minute you let your guard down, and that the sun will still rise in the morning, even on days when you decide to stay in bed. You can trust that no matter what happens, you have tried your best, and that you will continue to do so. You can even trust that, sometimes, trying your best means not trying at all.

# Acknowledgments

First and foremost, my agent, Kerry Sparks, who first encouraged me to write this book, and then championed it every step of the way. Your support and feedback have been invaluable.

A close second is my editor, Julie Will, who steered this book through some rough, rough drafts with patience, enthusiasm, and insight. Your expertise and intelligence are a huge part of what has given me the confidence to share such a personal story.

To Rebecca Rodd and Sydney Jeon, for being so on the ball and keeping everything on track, and to everyone at Flatiron Books and Levine Greenberg Rostan, for just generally being so all-around awesome.

To Lily Margison, for your willingness to do battle with the algorithm over and over (and over) again.

To my husband, for your unwavering support of my creative endeavors from day one, and for never doubting that my career and financial contributions to our family are just as important as yours. That's rare, and don't I know it. And thanks for doing the dishes, because I really, really hate the dishes.

To my son, for being the funniest, coolest, kindest person I know, and for just generally being the best thing to ever happen to me.

To all of the women who talked through this book with me, provided feedback, shared their own experiences and wisdom, and helped me believe this book was something I had to write, not just for myself, but for all of us.

And infinite gratitude to all the forces, seen and unseen, that have aligned to surround me with love and provide me with this opportunity. I do not take such blessings for granted.

## About the Author

**Kate Williams** is a former prom queen, yearbook editor in chief, and class president who's spent the last twenty years working in women's media in New York, Philadelphia, San Francisco, and Los Angeles. Her journalism has appeared in *Nylon*, *Elle*, and *Cosmopolitan*, among other publications, and she's worked behind the scenes for brands such as Urban Outfitters, Calvin Klein, and Nasty Gal. A *New York Times* bestselling ghostwriter, she has written seven uncredited books in addition to four young adult novels: the Babysitters Coven trilogy and the thriller *Never Coming Home*. Originally from Kansas, she now lives by the beach with her family of humans and animals and seizes every opportunity to nap.